GENERAL JOSEPH BLOOMFIELD

GENERAL
JOSEPH BLOOMFIELD

A Revolutionary Life

DONALD JOHNSTONE PECK

Flying Camp Press

an imprint of

AHP

American History Press

Staunton, Virginia

(888) 521-1789

Visit us on the Internet at:

www.Americanhistorypress.com

ISBN 13: 978-1-939995-06-3

Library of Congress Control Number: 2014952349

November 2014

Manufactured in the United States of America on acid-free paper. This book meets all ANSI standards for archival quality.

DEDICATION

This book is dedicated to the one person I know who has done the most to forward the preservation and promotion of the history and culture of Woodbridge Township, and whose loyalty, dedication and hard work are second to none—Dolores Capraro Gioffre, Ed.D.

CONTENTS

ACKNOWLEDGMENTS

I would like to acknowledge the following persons who, during my youth, inspired my interest in the colonial history of Woodbridge: The Reverend Earl H. Devanney, The Reverend William M. Justice and Martha Morrow.

I would also like to acknowledge the dedication of members of the Woodbridge Historic Preservation Commission with whom I served: Bruce Christensen, The Reverend Robert L. Counselman, Daniel D'Arcy, Dolores Capraro Gioffre, Ed.D., Kathy Jost-Keating, Courtney Lowry, Elizabeth Reeves, Wenda Rottweiler, Jane Sinnott, Elizabeth Stauffer, George W. Stillman, Sr., and Barbara Wyatt. I am also indebted to the current leadership of the Historical Association of Woodbridge Township: Daniel D'Arcy, Audrey and Frank LaPenta, Charles and Mary Ann Paul, Kathy Jost-Keating and long time members Emma Arrow, Catherine Burns, Helen Ringwood and Brenda Velasco.

My final acknowledgments are to James P. Egan, my longtime companion, C. Robert Kochek, who read the manuscript for accuracy, Gordon Bond, who researched and prepared the images for publication and David E. Kane, the publisher, whose final editing is very much appreciated.

Donald Johnstone Peck
Olde Stone Cottage
Fords, New Jersey
November 2014

PREFACE

Growing up in Woodbridge, New Jersey in the 1940s and '50s, I was always interested in the architecture of buildings, the exploration of known historic sites, and old roads and their locations. During my youth I walked to school to receive my primary and secondary education in Woodbridge public schools. This gave me time to observe and reflect on what I saw, and I always wished to learn more. My first awareness of the historic significance of Woodbridge came from my associations with the Methodist and Presbyterian churches and my high school history teacher, Martha Morrow. But I can honestly report that I have no recollection of ever learning about Joseph Bloomfield.

In recent years my association with both the Woodbridge Historic Preservation Commission and the Historical Association of Woodbridge Township have once again focused my attention on my hometown. The challenges faced for the benefit of present and future residents of Woodbridge Township by both of these fine organizations are inspiring to those of us who have labored to protect, promote and preserve our local history.

As it celebrates its 350th anniversary in 2014, it is important to acknowledge New Jersey both for the contributions it has made from the colonial era until present times, and also for the distinction of being named the *Crossroads of the American Revolution*. Due to its geographical location and strong individual patriot leadership, Woodbridge had a significant role to play in the success of the Revolution as well as the subsequent years in the development of New Jersey.

When remembering the state's role in the American Revolution, town names like Trenton, Princeton and Morristown come easily to mind, but Woodbridge does not. Those communities, as well as regions in nearby

Monmouth and Somerset Counties, have taken an active role in restoring their historic sites in order to tell their colonial and American Revolution stories. Woodbridge has sites, too, but they had not been seriously promoted until just recently.

I learned from my colleagues in the Woodbridge history community that a greater awareness of local history had to come from residents who really care about the community. In Woodbridge the Preservation Commission is well on its way to marking historic sites and establishing walking tour guides. The Historical Association of Woodbridge Township is making efforts to produce a local history museum and more publicized historic disclosure, making Woodbridge a destination point for historic tourism and the Crossroads of the American Revolution endeavor.

It is my hope that remembering the importance of the life and times of Joseph Bloomfield, an illustrious patriot son of Woodbridge, will add to the contribution of those who volunteer within our community to promote our history.

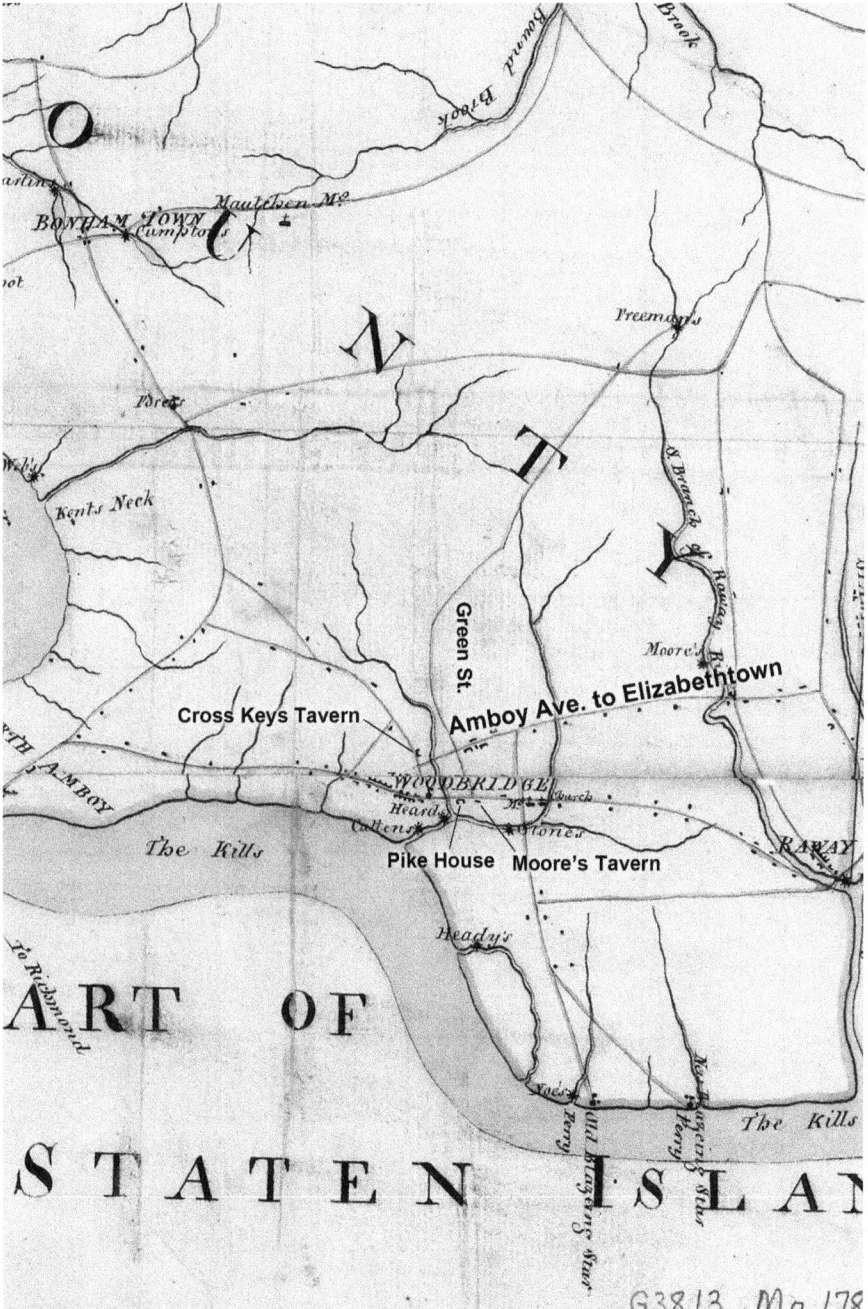

Woodbridge as it was mapped in 1781, from *"A map, Middlesex County. Reduced from the original survey by I. Hills, asst. engineer, 1781."* United States Library of Congress. Overlay based on research by Doug Wilson.

FOREWORD

As Mayor of Woodbridge Township—the oldest established township in the state of New Jersey—I receive many requests for public remarks, speeches, commentary, and interviews. The request from Donald Peck to author the Foreword for his latest historical narrative came as somewhat of a "curveball" from left field (speaking in baseball terms as a certified baseball aficionado and rabid New York Yankee fan).

I was somewhat skeptical, as the elected mayor, to even consider the request (notwithstanding my solid electoral base). However, the more I contemplated composing the Foreword, the more enthralled I became with Don's request, recognizing that I will ultimately have a place in the annals of Woodbridge history—not unlike Joseph Bloomfield—and that Don may someday decide that my place in history is worthy of his next historical endeavor.

Perhaps I should start with an introductory historical perspective (borrowed from a "Brief History of Woodbridge Township") I found on the township web page at www.twp.woodbridge.nj.us. Woodbridge was settled in the early autumn of 1664 and was granted a charter on June 1, 1669 by King Charles II of England. Joseph Dally, in his history of Woodbridge (*Woodbridge and Vicinity*, published 1873), records that it was so-called in honor of the Reverend John W. Woodbridge of Newbury, Massachusetts.

What we do know is that in the 1800s the large territory that made up Woodbridge Township was gradually divided, and portions of the area went to other municipalities. The original boundaries of Woodbridge Township were comprised of the communities we now know as Carteret, Rahway, New Dover, Oak Tree, Bonhamtown, Metuchen, Milton, Avenel, Colonia, Iselin, Menlo Park, Fords, Hopelawn, Keasbey, Sewaren, Port Reading, the eastern part of Raritan Township, and Woodbridge Proper.

In the old days, the familiar names for the various sections were Woodbridge, Blazing Star (sometimes called Rahway Neck, now the Borough of Carteret), Lower Rahway (now Rahway), Uniontown (now Iselin), Metuchen, Pleasant Mills (now designated as the Inman Avenue section of Colonia), Bonhamtown and Hills, and Florida Grove. Lower Rahway or Rahway became a part of Union County in 1860 by an act of the legislature. Ten years later, Raritan Township, now Edison Township, came into being and part of Piscataway and Metuchen, then a part of Woodbridge, went to make up that municipality. Finally, in 1906, a piece of land was taken away from Woodbridge to create the borough of Roosevelt, now Carteret.

So, there you have the geography. Today, the township stands as the fifth largest municipality in the state of New Jersey with some twenty-seven square miles and nearly 100,000 residents residing in the ten towns that we call Woodbridge Township: Avenel, Colonia, Fords, Hopelawn, Iselin, Keasbey, Menlo Park Terrace, Port Reading, Sewaren and Woodbridge.

But enough about our ten towns…let's get back to our author, Donald Johnstone Peck and General Joseph Bloomfield, Woodbridge's most famous citizen. Joseph Bloomfield led New Jersey in the development of our two party system by organizing the Republican Party of Thomas Jefferson and James Madison in New Jersey and then becoming New Jersey's first Republican governor.

Born into the aristocratic Woodbridge Bloomfield family, he distinguished himself as an officer in the American Revolution, as well as the War of 1812. He served as the mayor of Burlington, governor of New Jersey and two terms as a member of the U.S House of Representatives from New Jersey. As Woodbridge Township's most celebrated citizen, this story of Joseph Bloomfield highlights the importance of the township's colonial history and its important role as a member of New Jersey's Crossroads of the American Revolution National Heritage Area, connecting people and places of New Jersey's rich Revolutionary heritage to inspire community pride, stewardship and civic engagement (http://www.revolutionarynj.org/).

To the casual reader, *General Joseph Bloomfield – A Revolutionary Life* is an impressive historical account, but practitioners of local and regional history will be astonished by the book's depth of detail and complexity. The full story of the Bloomfield's contribution to Woodbridge—from Thomas Bloomfield, Sr., the original American pioneer ancestor and settler of Woodbridge, to Thomas Bloomfield, Jr., John Bloomfield, Ezekiel Bloomfield, Moses Bloomfield to Joseph Bloomfield and the ancestral line of Bloomfields today—is chronicled in exquisite detail that puts the reader at Joseph Bloomfield's dinner table.

Perhaps the most daunting challenge which faced author Peck during this work were the currents that swirl throughout Woodbridge Township's historical community. Maybe it's because we have so much history (much of which remains to be chronicled) that our Woodbridge historians take its history very seriously. (Any place which can call itself "the oldest established township in the state of New Jersey" with a straight face is very serious indeed.) However, with his Woodbridge Township passport in hand (growing up in Woodbridge in the 1940s and '50s) and his historical research skills honed to the finest edge, Donald Peck was able to traverse the Woodbridge Township historical landscape and complete the first full accounting of Joseph Bloomfield and the Bloomfield contribution to the make-up of what is Woodbridge Township today.

In as much as Woodbridge will celebrate its 350th anniversary in 2015, *General Joseph Bloomfield – A Revolutionary Life* is a wonderful and exacting introduction to the annals of Woodbridge history, standing as a significant testament and accounting of General Joseph Bloomfield.

From all of us who continue to flog away at the history of this remarkable Township—the oldest established in the state of New Jersey, "Thank You, Donald J. Peck!"

Mayor John E. McCormac
Township of Woodbridge
August 22, 2014

WOODBRIDGE, NEW JERSEY

Early Family History of the Bloomfields

Woodbridge, New Jersey, was the scene of major fighting between British Tories and American Continentals during the Revolutionary War. It may be named in honor of the pious Congregationalist clergyman, the Reverend John W. Woodbridge, born in Wiltshire, England, in 1613. A number of his associates and their families arrived in Woodbridge in the summer of 1665 from Newbury, Massachusetts, where they had first settled in 1635. Woodbridge passed away in 1691.

The harshness of New England's winters, its grubby farmland, and its constant religious bickering, among other causes, drove many colonists southward. The calm waters on Raritan Bay lured colonists off the stormy Atlantic and the placid Arthur Kill enticed them inland to settle near the then navigable Woodbridge River. Here they sought to continue their theocracy, which placed the Meeting House-Church, erected in 1675, at the center of their lives.

The Puritan settlers of Newbury, Massachusetts came primarily from Suffolk County, England, where the English town of Woodbridge is situated. It was a custom in New England to name towns after the localities in England from where the settlers had come from. According to William Whitehead, among the prominent settlers, mostly of Puritan heritage, coming from Newbury, Massachusetts were Daniel Pierce, John Pike, John Bishop, Henry Jacques, Hugh March, and Stephen Kent.

Joseph Bloomfield's original American pioneer ancestor and settler of Woodbridge, Thomas Bloomfield, Sr., descended from Thomas Bloomfield, a major in Oliver Cromwell's army. After finding himself on the losing side after Charles II was restored as king, Bloomfield fled to America.

English provincial governor Philip Carteret granted a charter to the 30,000-acre Township of Woodbridge on June 1, 1669, making it the oldest township in New Jersey. The earliest proprietors issued patents to actual settlers in 1670 for lands within the township. Among the original settlers from New England in 1667 was Thomas Bloomfield, a carpenter, who in 1670 was granted 326 acres. His son, Thomas Bloomfield, Jr. was granted 92 acres and John Bloomfield 90 acres. The Bloomfield family originated in Woodbridge, Suffolk, England. Thomas Bloomfield, Sr. arrived in Newburyport, Massachusetts in 1638, and he moved with his wife and family to Woodbridge, New Jersey in 1667.

The Township Court was established October 19, 1669, and in March of 1670 Thomas Bloomfield, Sr. was appointed a grand juryman. Both he and Thomas Bloomfield, Jr. became freeholders in 1670. Among the deputies to the General Assembly were Thomas Bloomfield, in 1675, and Ezekiel Bloomfield in 1676-78. Ezekiel was the great-grandfather of Governor Joseph Bloomfield.

By 1682 there were about 600 New England and Long Island Puritans settled in Woodbridge. By 1700 there was a growing, diverse population of English, Dutch, Flemish and Scottish settlers living side by side with them. Although the English outnumbered any other single group, by 1776 other nationalities, including slaves, were well represented. Gradually the Puritanism of Woodbridge broke down and the general cultures of East and West Jersey gained in similarity. New Jersey became a melting pot, a fusion of culture more typically American than that of New England or the South.

DR. MOSES BLOOMFIELD

Moses Bloomfield, the father of Joseph Bloomfield, was born in Woodbridge December 4, 1729. He was the son of Joseph Bloomfield and the grandson of Ezekiel Bloomfield, one of five children of Thomas Bloomfield, Sr. His wife was Sarah Ogden, the daughter of Robert and Phoebe Ogden of Elizabethtown, New Jersey. For forty years he was a practitioner of medicine of more than ordinary ability at Woodbridge and was considered one of the best physicians of his day. He was one of three physicians who organized the Medical Society of New Jersey July 23, 1766, and was active and efficient in its service. He was its secretary in 1767, and later it president in 1785.

Dr. Bloomfield was a representative in the colonial New Jersey Assembly and the Provincial Congress that replaced the assembly when independence from Great Britain was declared. He was commissioned as a surgeon at the United States Hospital in the Continental Army on May 14, 1777, was an upright magistrate and an elder in the local Presbyterian Church. He died on August 14, 1791. An obituary published in the *New Jersey Journal on* August 31, 1791 said: "He maintained an eminent character as a scholar, a physician and a Christian. He served in civil offices of trust and honor. He was benevolent and liberal to the poor, religious without bigotry. In his death the State has lost a worthy citizen and the Presbyterian Church an important member."

The Bloomfields' church was the First Presbyterian Church of Woodbridge, or Old White Church. It was situated on the old town green, as was the custom of its Puritan founders from New England. The present edifice was erected in 1803 and modified in 1972 to preserve its interior. The adjacent cemetery is one of the oldest in New Jersey. In the great congregation that lies buried here are the remains of many distinguished men and women, the Revolutionary heroes: Dr. Moses Bloomfield; Generals Nathaniel Heard and Clarkson Edgar; Colonels Samuel Crow and Benjamin Brown; Major Reuben Potter; Captains Nathaniel Fitz Randolph; David Edgar; Matthew Sayers; Ellis Barron and Abraham Tappan; Lieutenant James Paton; and a great host of the "rank and file."

Slavery had seemed as inherent a part of the world in which Moses Bloomfield was raised as the sun that rose every morning, and for years he had accepted it. For all their obvious and substantial presence, slaves were virtually invisible in early American history. What Moses Bloomfield's obituary notice didn't mention was that on July 4, 1783, at an historic antislavery meeting at his farm in Woodbridge, Moses Bloomfield freed his fourteen slaves. Dr. Bloomfield is reported to have told his slaves that inasmuch as a nation had declared that all men had the right to freedom, he could not consistently undo the principles of the Declaration of Independence by holding slaves.

For many of the founders, the freedom they sought did not extend to Blacks, who had no rights at all. George Washington, incidentally, was the only slave-owning president to free his slaves. The institution of slavery played an important role in the economy of the "Garden Colony" and later the "Garden State," since at least a third of the state lay south of the Mason-Dixon line. Although New Jersey finally passed an ordinance for gradual abolition, slavery in New Jersey would continue until 1847.

For colonial New Jerseyans in Woodbridge and elsewhere, life in the field was hard, and homes were cold and drafty. Granted a charter by King George II on September 8, 1756, the First Presbyterian Church of Woodbridge offered little cheer, either in its physical facility or during the long sermons of its ministers. By the mid-18th century the church took on a new meaning for its members, with the stirring revivalism of the Great Awakening, a period of increased religious enthusiasm. It reached an apex when the Reverend George Whitefield, a major proponent of the movement, toured the colonies in the 1740s. His visit was a source of revival to Presbyterians in Woodbridge, New Brunswick, and Newark, and as far south as Greenwich and Deerfield in Cumberland County. Religious in nature, promoting the freedoms of man in a civil society and the possibilities of what free men can do, the Great Awakening found a home in two major educational institutions of 18th century New Jersey—the College of New Jersey (later Princeton University) and Queens College (today's Rutgers University).

The Awakening had helped establish communication between a network of pastors and committees of correspondence with the independence-minded citizens throughout the colonies. Caught up in the evangelical mood of the period, Calvinist churches in the colonies replaced the sovereignty of the kings and Roman Catholic Church with the Bible and the sovereignty of God. It was god-given democratic rights that were preached from the pulpit. This doctrine of religious and political rights had language similar to the American Declaration of Independence and the Constitution. Rights, rights, and yet more rights were used to influence the political agenda of both the clergy and the politicians.

A popular song of that time, "The Contented Farmer," summed up the prevailing evangelical and independence-minded sentiment of that time:

> "What care I for affairs of state,
> or who is rich, or who is great.
> How far abroad ye Ambitious roam,
> to bring or Gold or Silver home:
> What is't to me, if France or Spain,
> Consent to Peace, or Wars maintain.
>
> I pay my taxes, Peace or War,
> and wish all well at Gibraltar,
> But mind a Cardinal no more
> Than any other Scarlet Whore:
> Grant me ye Pow'rs but health and rest,
> And let who will the world contest."

PRELUDE TO REVOLUTION

The Stamp Act

The flames of a spreading anti-Stamp Act sentiment were fanned by the appearance in New York of an anonymous single issue of a newspaper titled *The Constitutional Courant*. Dated September 21, 1765 and described as "the most remarkable of the inflammatory papers," the evidence pointed to it having come from the press of another famous Woodbridge son, James Parker. There was some mystery surrounding its production, and whether Parker was actually aware of his shop being used for such a controversial and possibly dangerous job. One of his journeymen, William Goddard, later admitted to having used the press belonging to his boss at Woodbridge. So there really wasn't any mystery after all.

An example of one of the stamps used to show the tax had been paid

The *Courant* proved to be a one-day wonder. It was considered so incendiary that New York printers—including Sons of Liberty supporter John Holt—refused to print it. A postrider claimed to have received the bundles from James Parker himself for delivery to New York, but there remains some question as to how involved Parker may have been. The single *Courant* issue declared itself to be "No Wise Repugnant to Loyalty," but it accused those behind the Stamp Act, due to take effect November first, of subverting the rights of freeborn Englishmen. An outraged New York Lt. Governor Cadwallader Colden appealed to Benjamin Franklin to examine the paper to see if it had indeed been printed

New York Lieutenant Governor Cadwallader Colden. *Harper's Encyclopedia of United States History, Harper & Brothers, 1905*

using the types of his friend and business partner, James Parker. Threats of mob violence, however, convinced them not to investigate further.

Protests and cries of taxation without representation occurred throughout the state. When the stamps arrived off New York on the HMS *Royal Charlotte*, Governor Franklin refused to let them be landed in Perth Amboy or New Jersey. Crowds in Woodbridge cheered Sons of Liberty speakers who vowed British subjects could be taxed "only by their own representatives." Word of the Stamp Act repeal reached New Jersey on April 3, 1766. In Woodbridge the Sons of Liberty combined a celebration of King George's birthday early

Portrait of The Rt. Hon.
Charles Townshend MP
(1725-1767) *Circa 1765*
by Joshua Reynolds

in June with a public observance of the Stamp Act repeal at the Liberty Oak
(location unknown) and presumably drank eighteen toasts while enjoying
roast ox, plum pudding, and cake—"and the most firm loyalty seemed to
glow in every breast."

In 1767 Parliament passed the Townshend Acts, a series of duties on glass,
paper, tea, and painter's supplies. This prompted the colonies to enact
various Non-importation Agreements, in which they promised to import
no more English goods. Woodbridge merchants announced their own
Non-importation Agreement on April 23, 1770. The town named twelve
merchants and twelve farmers to a Committee of Correspondence to notify
other New Jersey towns and the other colonies of their decision. They kept a
supply of tar and feathers near the center of town and a ducking stool handy
for anyone who might misunderstand the seriousness of non-importation.

JOSEPH BLOOMFIELD

Education at Deerfield Academy and with Cortlandt Skinner

Joseph Bloomfield, lawyer, soldier and governor, was born October 18, 1753, in the old Bloomfield family homestead, which is still standing on Harrell Avenue in Woodbridge. In that period near-illiteracy was the rule in most of New Jersey, since those were times of a simple agricultural economy, and higher education was not a necessity. Young Joseph had grown up with an appreciation of the performance of the typical chores on his father's large Woodbridge plantation, but was scarcely reconciled to them. He received his formal education at Deerfield Academy in South Jersey and acquired a quick grasp of the political issues that were leading to the Revolution. With a proclivity to become a jurist, he had almost finished reading law with Cortlandt Skinner when the Revolution began.

Joseph Bloomfield received his classical college preparatory education, which included Latin, under Reverend Enoch Green at his parsonage of the Deerfield Presbyterian Church in Deerfield, Cumberland County, roughly twelve miles to the north of Greenwich, New Jersey. Green was also active in the early anti-slavery movement that also appealed to Joseph Bloomfield. Much like Bloomfield's hometown of Woodbridge, Puritans from New England and Scots-Irish from Long Island had settled along both banks of the Cohansey River and founded the nearby port towns of Fairfield, Greenwich and Deerfield. Both of these groups were decidedly anti-British. The "New Lights" Presbyterian movement, an offshoot of the Great Awakening, influenced the Deerfield Church. The movement in general filled New Jersey Presbyterian churches with both religious and political revivalism.

Since there was no church in Bridgeton, also on the Cohansey River, Presbyterians in the vicinity traveled to the Deerfield Church. There were no Tories among these folks. After the start of the Revolutionary War on the green at Lexington, Massachusetts on April 19, 1775, the people of Bridgeton

The Bloomfield House as it appears today. *Photo courtesy Gordon Bond.*

Deerfield Presbyterian Church. *Wikipedia; Creative Commons License.*

became ardent supporters of the Revolution. A company of local militia was raised and many Presbyterians were among the volunteers, including Ebenezer Elmer, whose brother Jonathan, a lieutenant, was captained by Joseph Bloomfield, and later became a general and member of the U.S. Senate.

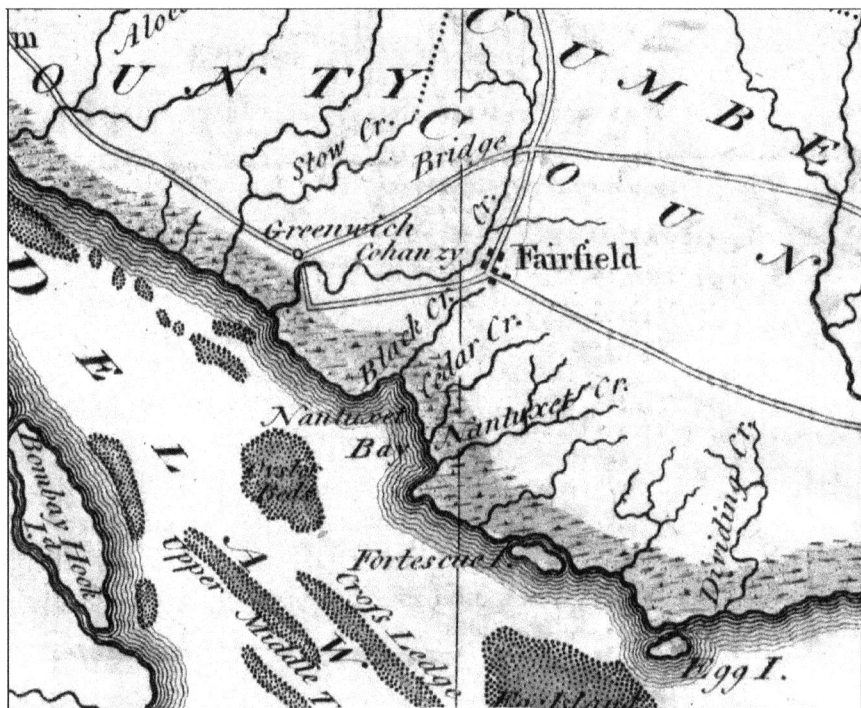

The Cohansey River area from a 1795 map of New Jersey. *"The State of New Jersey Compiled from the Most Authentic Information; Engraved for Carey's Edition of Guthries Geography Improved."* *Compiled by Samuel Lewis, engraved by W. Barker. Detail.*

Later, while a student of Cortlandt Skinner, Joseph Bloomfield would learn about many of the revolutionary issues that had first been debated when seventy-two New Jersey delegates from local Committees of Correspondence, including delegates from Woodbridge, met in New Brunswick on July 21, 1774 (without the permission of the governor, king or parliament). Their position was that they could not be taxed except by their own consent, given personally or by their representatives. In general, they found the imposition of taxes unconstitutional and oppressive.

The New Jersey delegates elected representatives to meet in September with commissioners from other colonies to organize the First Continental Congress in 1774 and the Second Continental Congress in 1775. At these meetings the delegates debated with the Loyalists, who were seeking a low profile as Patriot forces seized effective control of the government through the colony-wide New Jersey Provincial Congress and its Committee of Safety and Observation. Together they took charge of the affairs of the colony in place of the increasingly isolated royal governor and his officials.

Cumberland County, on the Delaware Bay, was also a Patriot hotbed, with the flames burning brightest in Bridgeton, the county seat. The town was also home to the *Plain Dealer*, one of the colony's first radical newspapers. Much like Joseph Bloomfield's hometown of Woodbridge, Bridgeton had a number of ranking officers and many enlisted men who served under Washington.

Joseph Bloomfield entered the office of Cortlandt Skinner in Perth Amboy in 1772. By the outbreak of the Revolution there were two young men, both students of the law, studying with Skinner. One was Andrew Bell, the son of a Perth Amboy British army officer, and the other was Joseph Bloomfield of Woodbridge. Bell embraced the Loyalist cause and eventually went with Cortlandt Skinner to New York in 1776, where he became one of the private secretaries to Sir Henry Clinton. Bell was with the British army in their retreat from Philadelphia across New Jersey, followed by the Battle of Monmouth. Joseph Bloomfield espoused the colonial cause and was with the American army during the Battle of Monmouth.

According to William A. Whitehead, a nineteenth century New Jersey historian, Cortlandt Skinner was the eldest of four sons of the Reverend William Skinner and Elizabeth, the youngest daughter of Stephanus Van Cortlandt of New York. William Skinner was the Fourth Rector of St. Peter's Church in Perth Amboy. Cortlandt was educated for the bar, studying the profession in the office of David Ogden, an old and distinguished practitioner at Newark, and practiced law for some time at Ogden's Newark office. In 1752 he married Elizabeth, daughter of Philip Kearny of Amboy, and took up residence in Amboy. He was appointed the king's Attorney General for the province in 1754 and held that office up to the time of the Revolution. Except for one year's sickness, he was also Speaker of the Assembly between 1765 and 1776.

After studying law under Cortlandt Skinner for two years, Joseph Bloomfield was admitted to the bar in November of 1774. He entered law practice in Bridgeton in February 1775, the same town where he had bonded with so many of the area patriots. His legal activities were sporadically interrupted by the war, and on February 7, 1776, the Provincial Congress appointed Joseph Bloomfield a captain in Colonel Dayton's Third New Jersey Regiment of Foot in the Continental Army. Improbably, his first duty was to arrest Cortlandt Skinner, but Skinner escaped the day before his planned arrest and took refuge aboard the HMS *Asia*, a Man-of-War then lying in the waters of New York Bay.

According to Whitehead, on April 2, 1776, Capt. Bloomfield's company of the Third Regiment of Jersey Blues troops arrived in Perth Amboy after crossing the Raritan River from South Amboy in the afternoon. Since Colonel Heard's Militia already occupied the British Barracks at Amboy, the Third Regiment was obliged to proceed to Woodbridge, and on to Eizabethtown the next day. On April 10 the company returned, and from that time until April 28—when they again marched into Elizabethtown— they were engaged in throwing up entrenchments in Perth Amboy under the direction of Major Francis Barber of the First Battalion. Joseph Bloomfield, a member of the Third Regiment, was also stationed in Perth Amboy during the summer of 1776 with the Flying Camp.

Promoted to the rank of major of the Third Regiment on November 28, 1776, Bloomfield was destined to be ordered to take part in the expedition against Canada in 1777. This regiment reached Albany, New York, learned of the Continental repulses at Quebec, and was dispatched to the Mohawk Valley to overawe the Indians. The following November, in 1777, it marched to Ticonderoga, and there Major Bloomfield was appointed Judge Advocate of the northern army.

THE EVE OF THE REVOLUTION

By the eve of the Revolution, Woodbridge was a popular stagecoach stop on the Upper Road, so its merchants profited from travelers from New York and New England who stopped at its taverns. Among these were the Elm Tree Tavern, the Pike House, and the most famous of them all, the Cross Keys Tavern, which was situated at the crossroads of the Upper Road and the King's Highway leading to the East Jersey capital city of Perth Amboy.

Traveling from Elizabethtown on the Old Dutch (or Upper) Road (today's Route 514), Woodbridge was on the main road between New York and Philadelphia. The Cross Keys Tavern, built in about 1740, was an important and regular meeting spot. Traveling to Philadelphia to help organize the

An early photo of the Cross Keys Tavern before it was moved *http://www.woodbridgetownshipnj. tripod.com/oldwoodbridgeimages/crosskeystavern1.jpg*

First Continental Congress in August of 1774, John Adams might well have stopped for refreshment here and shared his vehement anti-British sentiments. Woodridge Presbyterians of Puritan descent would certainly have been receptive to Adams' anti-British rhetoric.

Taverns were crowded each night with townsmen discussing current issues and listening intently to travelers who were passing through the area. Townsfolk now knew that war was imminent, and the Committees of Correspondence increased their letter exchanges. New Jersey had been the last colony to establish a Committee of Correspondence on February 8, 1774. It met on May 31, 1774, for the purpose of responding to an emergency message from the Boston Committee of Correspondence about the Port Act, which had closed Boston Harbor in retribution for the Boston Tea Party. Township Tories were strong in number and vocal in their opinions, but the Patriots outnumbered them. Their once-friendly neighbors ostracized the Loyalists in Woodbridge.

Travelers were the carriers of ideas, including opinions, thoughts, fads and serious political movements. Seditious talk in the Cross Keys' smoky taproom would have given the Bloomfield men of Woodbridge quite a bit to discuss at their dinner table. George Washington, who was appointed as Commander of the Continental Army on June 15, 1775, traveled through Middlesex County on the well established stagecoach route through Woodbridge later that month and certainly passed, and may have been entertained and refreshed at, the Cross Keys Tavern.

Quakers were early settlers of Woodbridge and organized their first meeting in a private home on August 17, 1689. They resided in Woodbridge until the outbreak of the Revolutionary War. The New Jersey legislature had exempted Quakers from military duty in 1705, and although they maintained outward neutrality in fact they tended to support allegiance to the crown. They continued to be persecuted for their pacifist position by local Patriots, and by 1776 they had been forced to move to Rahway and the Society of Friends Meeting house there for their own safety. In 1784 they sold their 1713 Woodbridge Meeting House to local Methodists.

The Jersey Blues, the oldest uniformed military militia organization in point of continuous service on the western continent, were organized in 1673 in

Woodbridge and Piscataway to control Native Americans from upper New York and Pennsylvania who came to the area during the summer months for fishing and often make a nuisance of themselves. When Independence was declared, many Woodbridge Township men joined the Jersey Blues who were stationed in Woodbridge, Piscataway and Perth Amboy. Local members, as well as boys who aspired to serve in the Blues, are believed to have held secret meetings at the homes of Timothy Bloomfield in the Fords section of Woodbridge Township and Joseph Gilman in Piscataway.

The First Continental Congress of 1774 at Philadelphia divided into moderate and radical camps, the later of which was led by New Englanders. It said nothing of independence. In New Jersey Loyalists objected to imperial taxes, but they believed in obedience to authority. They preferred to stress commercial and practical, rather than political, objectives to royal policies. The mood for complete severance was flamed in New Jersey by intemperate statements such as the one from Chief Justice Frederick Smyth of Perth Amboy who said, "People are guarding against imaginary tyranny, three thousand miles distant."

After the Boston Tea Party of December, 1774, Cortlandt Skinner supported the royal governor, William Franklin, who considered the Massachusetts acts ill-advised and through either the Bay Colony or the town of Boston should make compensation for the destroyed tea as a way of doing "Justice before they ask it of others." The effect of the First Continental Congress was to widen the breach between the mother country and the colonies. While William Franklin hoped to maintain a low profile and quietly wait out the current storm, that was not possible, since the legislature had not met since March, 1774 and governmental affairs required a meeting of the assembly on January 13, 1775.

In a masterful opening address, Franklin revealed his strategy. Stressing that he did not presume "to decide on the particular merits of the dispute between Great Britain and her Colonies" or intend "to censure those who conceive themselves aggrieved, for aiming at a redress of their grievances," Franklin declared that "All that I would wish to guard you against is the giving any Countenance or Encouragement to that destructive mode of proceeding which has been unhappily adopted in Part by some of the inhabitants of this Colony, and has been carried so far in others as totally to subvert their former Constitution." Should they approve extralegal protest activities, he warned, "you will do as much as lies in your Power to destroy that Form of Government of which you are an important Part, and which it is your Duty by all lawful means to preserve." Putting the assemblymen on the spot, he declared they must take the fork "evidently leading to peace, happiness, and a restoration of the public tranquility" or one "inevitably conducting you to anarchy, misery, and all the horrors of a civil war."

It appeared at first as if Franklin's forceful remarks would have the desired effect on the representatives, for most Jerseymen preferred moderation and restraint to radicalism. But members of the New Jersey congressional delegation quickly repaired to Perth Amboy to convince the assemblymen that a united front was essential to obtain satisfaction from the crown. On January 24, 1775, with a list of grievances which they forwarded to King George, the Assembly went on record in support of the proceedings of the Congress. Obviously Cortlandt Skinner and William Franklin were not happy about this. Joseph Bloomfield had much to contemplate, as did his father, Dr. Moses Bloomfield.

Whatever the circumstances, William Franklin's analysis of the political situation was correct. The British government dispatched military and naval reinforcements in preparation for a military contingency. When British regulars and American militiamen exchanged shots across Lexington green on April 19, 1775, the war that would have broken out sooner or later was on, and the time for talk had ended. Not until April 24, 1775, did a breathless post rider bring the astounding news to Woodbridge that British forces and the Minutemen of Massachusetts had clashed at Lexington five days earlier. When this news reached patriot leader Dr. Moses Bloomfield, he declared that the inhabitants of his hometown were "determined to stand or fall with the liberties of America." By late fall the New Jersey Provincial Congress had replaced the Assembly as the source of effective government in the colony.

The question facing all Americans was not who has the power, but who *should* have the power. During the past fifty years or so, the small landowner or yeoman farmer had become highly suspicious of the ruling elite, whose agenda was to frame the struggle for office and power to benefit only themselves. Arguments like "liberty" and "freedom" helped promote a soldier class to fight. All the same, one third of the population was pro-

Patriot, one third pro-British and the balance indecisive at the outbreak of the war.

While Moses Bloomfield's son reflected his parents' Puritan values and his aristocratic country gentleman upbringing, he was to pursue another destiny his father might not have predicted, as a member of the military and participant in politics. Joseph Bloomfield's desire for justice made it unreasonable to abandon the search for social and political solutions toward a higher order of being. His elite background, revolutionary service, inherited wealth and urbanity all propelled him toward Patriot political leadership at a time when many in his class had chosen to side with the Loyalists.

THE GREENWICH TEA PARTY

Joseph Bloomfield's Defense of Tea Party Activists

During this time, when relations between Great Britain and her Western Hemisphere colonies were deteriorating, boycotts were organized and cries of taxation without representation could be heard in Boston, Philadelphia and New Jersey. Captain Allen, the master of the English brig *Greyhound*, learned of resistance to his planned arrival in Philadelphia by the Sons of Liberty. On December 12, 1774, the brig, with a cargo of tea owned by the East India Company, unexpectedly put in at the port town of Greenwich, about five miles up the Cohansey River, not far from Bridgeton.

By 1750 Greenwich had evolved into a major shipping port, one of three legal ports of entry during that period, the others being Perth Amboy and Burlington. The tea was consigned to Philadelphia, but the skipper decided that the Greenwich cellar of Tory Daniel Bowen would be a safer storehouse. Feelings against the Townsend Duties by local Whigs were as high as they were in Boston. Angered by the arrival of the tea, they met in Bridgeton to discuss further action. Before any decision was reached, a group of younger men rounded up a band of forty from the nearby towns of Bridgeton, Fairfield, Shiloh, and Roadstown. Among them was Richard Howell, later to become the third governor of New Jersey.

Reminiscent of the "Mohawks" at the Boston Tea Party a year earlier, these local Whigs, disguised as Indians, marched on Greenwich, broke into Bowen's cellar and carried the chests to a roaring bonfire that soon lit up the village. The crackling flames and fragrant smoke aroused the whole town. Patriot exultation was not unmixed with regret at the loss of millions of good drinks; indeed, one of the tea burners, named Stacks, could not help stuffing handfuls of leaves into his close-fitting breeches. Before long his added bulk was noticed, and from then on to the end of his life he was known as "Tea" Stacks.

This monument was erected to commemorate the "Tea Burners" of the Greenwich Tea Party, the last of several such protests against the tax on tea, of which the Boston Tea Party is the best-known. *Photo courtesy Gordon Bond*

Tory sympathizers complained bitterly about the tea burning, and the English shippers finally started a court action against seven of the young Whig arsonists. The early local historian, Robert Gibbon Johnson, relates that Chief Justice Frederick Smyth of Perth Amboy, a close acquaintance of Cortlandt Skinner, twice charged a grand jury on the tea burning, but each time the jurors reported no bills "for this plain reason—they were Whigs." Seven of the arsonists were tried in April, 1775 and the young lawyer Joseph Bloomfield represented them. Their verdict of innocence surprised no one; Cumberland County was in no mood to punish tea burners.

Agriculture dominated Cumberland life well before the county became looked on as a wartime food supplier. Aware of Cumberland's patriotism, General Washington declared that if it hadn't been for the provisions sent by Cumberland and Salem counties to feed his troops at Valley Forge he would have had no army to continue the war.

THE DECISIVE YEAR OF 1776

In the spring of 1775, the New Jersey militia took uncommon pains to perfect themselves with military discipline; one company marched by the governor's mansion in Perth Amboy in May with "Colours, Drum and Fife." The fiery words of Thomas Paine's scorching political pamphlet *Common Sense*, published in January 1776, together with Royal Governor Franklin being placed on parole, further persuaded Joseph Bloomfield to espouse the Patriot cause. By January 8, 1776 William Franklin and Cortlandt Skinner had become marked men. At 2 a.m. on that day a "large party of men armed with guns and bayonets" under the command of Lieutenant Colonel William Winds put William Franklin under house arrest.

On the same day that the Continental Congress learned of William's arrest, the first copies of *Common Sense*, printed at Benjamin Franklin's suggestion, came off the press. The firebrand best seller was read in front of tens of thousands of American hearthsides that winter, making fence sitters shake their heads. Loyalists fumed and radicals demanded independence. The king of England was referred to as "the royal brute." Monarchy was "exceedingly ridiculous." The ancient ties between America and England "sooner or later must have an end." Cortlandt Skinner fled in exile and Joseph Bloomfield was glad that he had made his decision to join the rebel forces.

The minutes of the Board of Proprietors of the Eastern Division of New Jersey, dated April 13, 1776, recorded that "Mr. Skinner now absent and likely to continue so for some time," was an oblique reference to the fact that he was then with the Loyalist forces in New York City.

General Sir William Howe soon thereafter appointed Skinner a brigadier general with authority to raise five battalions from among the disaffected citizens of New Jersey. When Howe first occupied New York, he was told "New Jersey is a region overflowing with loyal adherents to the crown who only wait a safe opportunity to declare themselves." At first Howe believed this, but by early 1777 Skinner, headquartered on Staten Island, had only recruited 517 men and by May, 1778, the peak total had only increased to a mere 1,001 soldiers.

General Washington had to cope with the prospect of a British invasion of New Jersey. There were any number of good landing places for this to happen. Elizabethtown, Woodbridge and Perth Amboy were particularly vulnerable, since they were directly across from British-held Staten Island. While at the King's Arms Tavern at Perth Amboy on May 22, 1776, Washington dispatched eight regiments from his already-meager force to protect this exposed coastline in order to prevent a British strike from New York into the New Jersey interior. A landing here would put the British on a good road system and on the shortest route between their base in New York City and rebel-controlled Philadelphia.

In June of 1776, at Washington's urging, the Continental Congress in Philadelphia voted to raise companies from Maryland, Delaware and Pennsylvania to form a mobile service called The Flying Camp under Brigadier General Hugh Mercer, a military grouping poised to repel any British advance into New Jersey.

In the short space of the twelve years between 1763 and 1775, the ties that had bound Great Britain to her American colonies had become severely torn by those seeking political independence. Through it all, William Franklin remained profoundly loyal to King George III. In June 1776 the Continental Congress declared William Franklin "...an enemy to the liberties of this country..." They then ordered the Woodbridge innkeeper, Colonel Nathaniel Heard, to arrest the governor. Heard had already earned himself the name of "Tory hunter" for his brutal tactics in rounding up and disarming nearly 1,400 Loyalists on Long Island. To the tune of "Yankee Doodle" they bitterly sang:

Colonel Heard has come to town
In all his pride and glory;
And when he dies he'll go to Hell
For robbing of the Tory.

In handwritten orders empowering Heard to seize William Franklin "with all the delicacy and tenderness which the nature of the business can possibly admit," the Provincial Congress offered Franklin a parole, and the option to sit out the impending war in a town of his choosing, or submit to arrest. The governor scorned the parole.

On June 19, 1776, he was arrested by the Middlesex County Militia under the command of Colonel Heard, an old family friend of Joseph Bloomfield. Heard was under orders from Samuel Tucker, president of the Provincial Congress of which Moses Bloomfield was a member. Heard and a guard of sixty men had marched from the British Barracks in Perth Amboy to the Proprietary House and captured the beleaguered governor on the front steps. To Benjamin Franklin, the governor's father, it was the hour of his family's deepest disgrace.

Oddly enough, on June 20, 1776, Joseph Bloomfield's classmate Philip Fithian, who had studied with him at Rev. Enoch Green's Deerfield Academy, entered the service as a chaplain. He became a part of General Heard's brigade assigned to the defense of New York.

In Philadelphia, on June 21, congressional delegate Thomas Jefferson of Virginia delivered his first draft of the Declaration of Independence for John Adams of Massachusetts to review, including the phrase "We hold these truths to be self-evident, that all men are created equal, that they are endowed by their Creator with certain unalienable Rights, that among these are Life, Liberty and the pursuit of Happiness." Jefferson had the best of editors in private: the words 'self-evident" were Benjamin Franklin's addition. On the same date a court which he refused to recognize tried Franklin, and also on that day the New Jersey Provincial Congress voted 53-3 to declare independence from Great Britain.

Leading the Flying Camp with his Third Virginia Regiment, General Hugh Mercer marched into Perth Amboy and was soon headquartered at the Proprietary House with his officers, future President James Monroe and future Chief Justice John Marshall, just after Royal Governor William Franklin had been removed.

Thomas Jefferson. *Painting by Rembrandt Peale, 1800*

John Adams. *Painting by Asher B. Durand, Naval Historical Center, Washington, D.C.*

Benjamin Franklin. *Painting by Joseph Siffred Duplessis.*

With the Declaration of Independence adopted by Congress on July 4, 1776, war had officially begun. Many Americans did not want independence, and this was especially true in Perth Amboy, the official center of British domination in East Jersey. Here were the leading officers of the East Jersey Board of Proprietors, who favored the British government which had given them so much power and wealth. Prominent lawyers, doctors and merchants, along with Anglican clergy, assailed the split with the mother county.

By 1776 the population exhibited a religiosity of refugee faith across a kaleidoscope of denominations and sects. There was the religious intensity of seventeenth-century Puritans, Presbyterian Covenanters, early Dutch or Swiss Calvinists from Britain and Europe helping to stamp the North American colonies as a religious refuge. These included English and Welsh Puritans, Baptists, and Quakers. There were also French Huguenots, and a myriad of German speakers fleeing continental wars. These included Moravians, Palatines, Amish, Mennonites, Anabaptists, Dunkers, and Salzburgers, especially in the middle colonies. Their individualistic and anti-

The Proprietary House in Perth Amboy, NJ is the only official surviving royal governor's mansion in the original Thirteen Colonies. *Photo courtesy Gordon Bond*

James Monroe. *Painting by Samuel F. B. Morse*   John Marshall. *Painting by Henry Inman, 1832*

hierarchical faith emphasized a personal relationship with God. This made them responsive to pioneering evangelists; this was especially true among the Presbyterian and Dutch Reformed churches of New Jersey.

Presbyterian patriots of the stature of William Livingston, Richard Stockton III, Francis Hopkinson, William Alexander, John Witherspoon, Azel Roe, Moses and Joseph Bloomfield and a large number of young lawyers and intellectuals, along with the clergy of the Presbyterian and Dutch Reformed churches preaching independence from the pulpit, stood firmly for independence. The most notable preacher was the Reverend John Witherspoon. A lineal descendant of John Knox, he was born in Scotland in 1722 and came to America in 1768 to become the president of Princeton College, and later became a signer of the Declaration of Independence. In many New Jersey patriot circles the Revolution was now being called "The Presbyterian War."

Rev. John Witherspoon.
Wikipedia; Creative Commons License

While religious revolutionaries could hardly have envisioned an incipient theocracy in the twenty-first century bearing any resemblance to Calvin's Geneva or Winthrop's Massachusetts Bay Colony, neither could they have envisioned their Biblical inherency, religious fervor and the exaltation of faith over reason positions dominating politics. Politicians would continue to organize evangelical churches for their political purposes, and this continues to the present day.

The tide of the war had really turned by June 29, 1776, when one hundred of Lord Howe's transports dropped anchor off Sandy Hook. In Perth Amboy men of fighting age slipped away at night to join Cortlandt Skinner, who was forming a Loyalist regiment on Staten Island. George Washington wrote, "It is not un-likely that in a little time they may attempt to cross to the Jersey side, and induce many to join them… unless there is a force to oppose them." Washington ordered Hugh Mercer's Flying Camp to arrest the former Chief Justice Frederick Smyth, and other leading Perth Amboy Loyalists, and then march them to Princeton.

William Howe. *Mezzotint by Richard Purcell aka Charles Corbutt. From the Anne S.K. Brown Military History Collection at Brown University.*

By July 4, George Washington was worried that the thousands of redcoats already "marching about" nearby Staten Island "...are leaving no arts unassayed to gain the inhabitants to their side." "The disaffection of that place, and others not far distant, is exceedingly great, and unless it be checked and overawed it may become more general and very alarming," he communicated to Congress. The Patriots of Woodbridge were certainly alarmed, since their farms were ripe for foraging. Woodbridge was a particular hot bed for Patriots, and at the time included Carteret, Metuchen and parts of present-day Rahway and Edison Township.

Nathaniel Heard of Woodbridge was later named a brigadier general commanding, and finally a brigadier general of militia. In 1775 he raised a body of troops, which he placed at the disposition of the Provincial Congress and Committee of Safety. He was colonel of the first Middlesex regiment, and afterwards a colonel of a battalion of Minutemen. Later he was in command of a battalion named in his honor—Heard's Battalion. As the Loyalists were so firmly entrenched in Perth Amboy and Staten Island at that time, General George Washington sent word to Heard in July to arrest "any of the Amboy or Staten Island Tories who made themselves obnoxious to the cause of liberty."

On July 12, 1776, Lord Howe landed 15,000 of his troops on Staten Island. During that summer some 479 ships disgorged ordinance, supplies and some of the world's toughest troops into the area. Hessian forces were posted at Billop's Point, directly across the Arthur Kill from Perth Amboy. General Mercer struggled as he sought to organize his command, since militia companies arrived and departed almost daily, with the result that no orderly troop disposition could be made.

As the weeks dragged by without the anticipated attack from Staten Island, the men became restless and clamored to return to their homes and farms. Having spent the summer of 1776 with General Mercer in Perth Amboy, Thomas Paine characterized many of these men while writing during the Long Retreat from Fort Lee to Trenton, New Jersey between November 20, 1776 and December 8, 1776:

"These are the times that try men's souls. The summer soldier and the sunshine patriot will, in this crisis, shrink from the service of their country; but he that stands by it now deserves the love and thanks of man and woman."

Thomas Paine, along with Joseph Bloomfield, had later joined Washington's small army at Fort Lee. On their retreat along the muddy roads passing through Woodbridge after the British invasion, he had limped along while scribbling in his notebook on a drumhead that served as his desk. Paine's words, icons of American prose, comprised his series of sixteen pamphlets: *The American Crisis*. Many of the men he referred to were New Jersey troops, the vast majority of whom were farmers, many from Woodbridge, who had been temporarily excused to harvest hay in their sun-baked fields.

Thomas Paine. *Painting by Auguste Millière, after an engraving by William Sharp, after George Romney.*

Among the famous with whom Joseph Bloomfield associated in Perth Amboy during his Flying Camp service was Thomas Paine. His work *Common Sense*, the forty-seven-page pamphlet that cost two shillings, had begun selling on the streets of Philadelphia in January 1776, and had sold 120,000 copies three months later. At thirty-nine years of age, Paine became the plain-speaking voice of the Revolutionary cause. *Common Sense* was followed by *The Crisis*, which Paine wrote while traveling with the Continental Army during George Washington's retreat across New Jersey following the British invasion of New Jersey at Fort Lee on November 20, 1776.

Sometime in late July, using oxen, some Flying Camp militiamen from Woodbridge moved an old eighteen-pound swivel gun and planted it between breastworks in Perth Amboy's St. Peter's Churchyard. They then proceeded to open fire on a British man-o-war anchored in Raritan Bay. The frigate returned fire, shooting a hole in the gravestone of Gertrude Hay and damaging the gravestone of Captain William Bryant, a fragment of which can still be seen in the churchyard today.

The *American* CRISIS.

NUMBER I.

By the Author of COMMON SENSE.

THESE are the times that try men's fouls : The fummer foldier and the funfhine patriot will, in this crifis, fhrink from the fervice of his country ; but he that ftands it NOW, deferves the love and thanks of man and woman. Tyranny, like hell, is not eafily conquered ; yet we have this confolation with us, that the harder the conflict, the more glorious the triumph. What we obtain too cheap, we efteem too lightly :---'Tis dearnefs only that gives every thing its value. Heaven knows how to fet a proper price upon its goods ; and it would be ftrange, indeed, if fo celeftial an article as FREEDOM fhould not be highly rated. Britain, with an army to enforce her tyranny, has declared, that fhe has a right (*not only to* TAX, but) "to " BIND *us in* ALL CASES WHATSOEVER," and if being *bound in that manner* is not flavery, then is there not fuch a thing as flavery upon earth. Even the expreffion is impious, for fo unlimited a power can belong only to GOD.

WHETHER the Independence of the Continent was declared too foon, or delayed too long, I will not now enter into as an argument ; my own fimple opinion is, that had it been eight months earlier, it would have been much better. We did not make a proper ufe of laft winter, neither could we, while we were in a dependent ftate. However, the fault, if it were one, was all our own ; we have none to blame but ourfelves*. But no great deal is loft yet ; all that Howe has been doing for this month paft is rather a ravage than a conqueft, which the fpirit of the Jerfies a year ago would have quickly repulfed, and which time and a little refolution will foon recover.

I have as little fuperftition in me as any man living, but **my**

---

* "" The prefent winter" (meaning the laft) "' is worth an " age if rightly employed, but if loft, or neglected, the whole " Continent will partake of the evil ; and there is no punifh- " ment that man does not deferve, be he who, or what, or " where he will, that may be the means of facrificing a feafon " fo precious and ufeful." COMMON SENSE.

The American Crisis Number 1.

COMMON SENSE;

ADDRESSED TO THE *W. Hamilton*

INHABITANTS

OF

AMERICA,

On the following interesting

SUBJECTS.

I. Of the Origin and Design of Government in general,
with concise Remarks on the English Constitution.

II. Of Monarchy and Hereditary Succession.

III. Thoughts on the present State of American Affairs.

IV. Of the present Ability of America, with some mis-
cellaneous Reflections.

Thomas Paine

Man knows no Master save creating HEAVEN,
Or those whom choice and common good ordain.

THOMSON.

PHILADELPHIA;

Printed, and Sold, by R. BELL, in Third-Street.

MDCCLXXVI.

Common Sense.

By mid-August, a total of some 35,000 British and Hessian troops, the largest expeditionary force ever sent overseas prior to the great embarkations and landings of World Wars I and II, were stationed on Staten Island. On August 22, 1776, the Howes landed 15,000 of their Staten Island troops near the narrows off Long Island and engaged the Americans in the Battle of Long Island. After an abortive attempt to make peace on September 11 at the Conference House at Billop's Point, Staten Island, the British drove the Americans out of Manhattan and Westchester counties and into New Jersey.

In the fall of 1776, with the increased sniper attacks by the British from Staten Island, the Americans constructed small redoubts (entrenchments) along the embankment of Perth Amboy facing Staten Island to protect them from attack. Captain Bloomfield's company had earlier that year constructed a similar earthwork capable of holding 200 men, called the "Lower

The Christopher Billop house on Staten Island, also known as the Conference House, was site of the aborted peace talks on September 11, 1776 between the Americans and England. *Wikipedia; Creative Commons License.*

Entrenchment," in the vicinity of State Street and the old Presbyterian Graveyard (site of the present day McGinnis Middle School).

On November 20, the British invaded New Jersey at Fort Lee. Washington subsequently moved his troops south through Newark. Woodbridge was among those towns along the route that witnessed George Washington's troops marching on the road from Elizabethtown to New Brunswick, called the Upper Road, or sometimes the Old Dutch Road, as they passed through Rahway, Woodbridge and Piscataway in retreat. The day before passing through Woodbridge, in the early morning hours of November 29, Joseph Bloomfield was promoted to the rank of major. Closely pursuing the Americans and leaving Woodbridge on November 30, Lord Cornwallis ordered his troops to march to New Brunswick, awaiting further orders from Sir William Howe.

Washington wrote to Congress from New Brunswick, describing the drama and urgency of the situation: "I am now to inform you that the enemy are still advancing and that their vanguard has proceeded as far as Bonems (Bonhamtown), a small town about four miles this side of Woodbridge. All the men of the Jersey Flying Camp under General Heard.... refused to continue longer in service." General Howe's initial decision not to pursue the Americans beyond the Raritan River delayed Cornwallis's pursuit of the Americans and allowed Washington and his troops to escape to Pennsylvania.

By December 8, with Washington and the remnants of his Continental Army now in Pennsylvania, the British invasion of New Jersey was complete. Sir William Howe then ordered Lord Cornwallis to set up garrisons in an 80-mile line or "chain of posts" in Trenton, Princeton, New Brunswick, Perth Amboy, and Elizabethtown to hold the central part of New Jersey. The British gave up Elizabethtown, and also Woodbridge, and made their principal cantonments from December 1776 to June 1777 at the provincial capital of Perth Amboy, with their field headquarters at New Brunswick. If only Howe had known that Washington, encamped across the Delaware River, was busy watching Colonel Rall and his Hessian soldiers at Trenton like a hungry fox eyeing the chicken coop!

To the British, the American rebellion seemed on the verge of collapse by mid-December, 1776. Fearing the British would now seize Philadelphia, the

First Marquis of Cornwallis. *Painting by John Singleton Copley.*

Continental Congress fled to Baltimore and remained there until March 1777. Crown forces were in possession of New York City, Newport, Rhode Island and Perth Amboy. Many New Jersey citizens had accepted Howe's

The Tempe Wick House. *Historic American Buildings Survey 1939, Thomas T. Waterman, photographer.*

offer of pardon and hundreds of Loyalists were enlisting in the Provincial Regiment of Perth Amboy's Cortlandt Skinner.

American troop morale was low and troop desertion became a major concern. Washington glumly reported that many of his men were "entirely naked and most so thinly clad as to be unfit for service." He wrote to Congress "Ten more days will put an end to the existence of our army." But using the intelligence available to him, Washington planned his Christmas night strike on Trenton and, as we all know from our history books, the Americans soundly won the battle.

The Battle of Trenton was one of Washington's most incredible victories. General Howe, in New York, was stunned. He ordered Cornwallis to "bag the fox"; Cornwallis quickly landed some 8,000 troops at Perth Amboy and marched them on New Brunswick Avenue through Fords to Princeton. But Washington won again at the Second Battle of Trenton and followed his victory the next day at the Battle of Princeton on January 3, 1777, giving the nation new hope.

Washington's army then settled into winter headquarters at Morristown, New Jersey. Joseph Bloomfield, who had fought with Oliver Cromwell, the celebrated African-American Revolutionary War soldier, at the Battle of Trenton, was quartered at the Wick House at Jockey Hollow during the winter of 1777.

BRITISH CONTROL OF NEW JERSEY
IN 1777

From December of 1776 through June of 1777 the Township of Woodbridge was overrun by British and Hessian mercenaries who were foraging and looting, searching for needed meat, milk and produce. Horses, cattle and supplies of all kinds were regularly lost to the British. In early December, 1776, the Redcoats rounded up 400 head of cattle and 200 sheep in Woodbridge. They planned to feed the troops with them during the winter, but a wily militia appeared on the night of December 11 and quietly herded "John Bull's beef and mutton into a colonial camp."

Spirited homemaker Grace Lacky was horrified that Hessian soldiers were entering private homes in Woodbridge and stealing anything they could carry away. By writing the words "SMALL POX" in large letters on her front door, she was able to scare away her uninvited guests.

Indignant citizens in every town had tales of woe about how the British and Hessians robbed their homes. A sampling of losses suffered in Woodbridge included: "weather-boards stripped off a house, 2 Common Bibles, 1 Testament, and 1 Psalm Book, a Negro boy 12 years of age and a new pare of Leather Britches."

Continentals and Redcoats fought several skirmishes on Woodbridge soil in the spring of 1777. The successes at Trenton and Princeton enlivened the spirits of the Jersey Militia, and by January 5, 1777, under General William Maxwell, they were able to drive the British down the Short Hills through Woodbridge back to Perth Amboy.

On February 1, General Maxwell's militia again engaged foraging Royal forces on King Georges Post Road near Fords in the Battle of Spunk Hill. On

February 23, fifteen hundred British soldiers marched out of Perth Amboy and proceeded through Woodbridge to Rahway, only to be driven back once again by Maxwell's forces.

On March 8, two thousand Redcoats left Perth Amboy to attack the rebels in the Rahway camps, only to find that they had walked into a "nest of American hornets" at an engagement at Woodbridge's Strawberry Hill. Joseph Bloomfield, as an officer in the New Jersey Brigade, carried a fusil, or musket. In one fight against British raiders in Woodbridge on March 30, 1777, he reported that he "Fired eight Rounds myself being the first time I was ever in an action or saw the Enemy in the Field."

The heroine of Woodbridge was a zealous patriot named Janet Pike Gage. She is credited with having raised the first Liberty Pole with the "Stars and Stripes" in front of the Cross Keys Tavern in Woodbridge. On or about April 20, 1777, a young woman passing a vacant house in Woodbridge, who may have been Janet Gage, saw through its window a drunken Hessian soldier who had strayed from his party. There being no men within less than a mile of the town, she quickly returned, dressed in man's apparel, armed herself with an old firelock, returned to the house, entered it, and took control of the Hessian prisoner. She then stripped him of his arms and led him off to the parole guard of the New Jersey regiment stationed near Woodbridge.

After occupying Perth Amboy and New Brunswick from December 1776 through June 1777 following the Battle of the Short Hills, General Sir William Howe moved his entire force to Staten Island, burning and pillaging along their route. On July 23, he began embarking his troops on a magnificent armada of more than 250 warships destined not for Charleston, South Carolina, as had been expected, but rather to the head of the Chesapeake Bay within an easy march of Philadelphia.

General Sir William Howe's forces invaded the "rebel capital" of Philadelphia on September 26, 1777, via the Chesapeake Bay, after successfully engaged the Americans at Brandywine Creek and Paoli on September 11, 1777. He later fought them on October 4 at Germantown, Pennsylvania.

From Brandywine Joseph Bloomfield wrote: "I was wounded, having a Ball with the Wad (probably cartridge paper) shot through my left forearm…A stranger dressed my wound with some tow from my catorich (cartridge) box, & wrapped my Arm in my handkerchief." *Tow* was a coarse bundled fiber used for cleaning firearms and occasionally as wadding, and the fact that Bloomfield was wearing a cartridge box indicates he was carrying a musket or fusil.

A cannonball at the Battle of Brandywine beheaded Bloomfield's friend James Witherspoon, son of the John Witherspoon, Signer of the Declaration of Independence. The Marquis de la Fayette was shot through the leg during the same battle while rallying Lord Stirling's division of New Jersey and Pennsylvania troops.

As a result of American General Horatio Gates's victory at Saratoga on October 17, 1777 and the diplomacy of Benjamin Franklin, France signed treaties with the Americans in February, 1778 boosting confidence in the Patriot cause. The French alliance was a decisive one for the cause of American independence, and no American should ever forget that.

With the threat of the French blocking the naval supply route to Philadelphia, Sir Henry Clinton was ordered to take the British army back to New York City. Washington would now move his bedraggled troops from their winter headquarters at Valley Forge for a June, 1778, rendezvous with the British in New Jersey.

THE BATTLE OF MONMOUTH

Beginning at Valley Forge

G eneral Howe and his regiments led a relative life of comfort in Philadelphia during the winter of 1777-78. The Continental Army's time at Valley Forge, on the other hand, had been productive, despite their being characterized as "a ragged army." Prussian volunteer Baron von Steuben had proceeded to teach the new army how to march and maneuver and techniques to use bayonets effectively. That winter George Washington created an army of soldiers committed to winning the war, not leaving as soon as a short-term enlistment ran out. The suffering that all of the soldiers experienced during their encampment created an *esprit de corps*. Washington had fought ferociously to feed and clothe his men and to create a professional army, and by spring they were ready for action.

Washington had chosen Valley Forge as his winter encampment because of its proximity to Philadelphia—and to satisfy Pennsylvania politicians. He also chose Valley Forge to block the road to York, to spy on British General Sir William Howe and to be ready to act if the British moved, as well as to attack and harry British foragers. The Valley Forge location was also helpful in interfering with farmers bringing supplies to Philadelphia, where the British, who had plenty of ready cash, would pay a good price for them. Valley Forge was the place where the true Continental Army was born.

Hunger and deprivation, bloody footprints left in the snow by shoeless soldiers, an encampment ravaged by disease—that was Valley Forge. The Congressional supply system had improved for a while, but by the time Martha Washington arrived in February from Mount Vernon, soldiers were again on the verge of starvation. They were no longer freezing in tents, but they needed a regular food supply.

Major General Friedrich Wilhelm Augustus Baron von Steuben. *Painting by Ralph Earl. Yale University Art Gallery.*

Housed in the wooden barracks they had constructed, their rags and tatters a joke as they huddled about roaring fires, the troops had at least located plenty of wood and ample water. Surrounded by farms in all directions,

General Washington and Lafayette look over the troops at Valley Forge. *Library of Congress.*

American foragers began supplying the camp from those farms, much to their owners' displeasure.

Meanwhile, the British army lived comfortably in Philadelphia. Howes' 20,000 soldiers (to Washington's original 11,000 to 12,000, decreased by some 2,500 deaths over the course of the winter) had settled in for the season, enjoying themselves tremendously. A Hessian captain wrote, "Assemblies, Concerts, Clubs and the like make us forget that there is any war, save that it is a capital joke." British officers organized a very good amateur theatre, acting in it along with their mistresses. Food and drink were plentiful for an army with hard cash to spend, and the merchants of the town were happy to comply.

Right behind Martha, the Baron von Steuben, a Prussian professional soldier with a self-bestowed title and rank, had arrived at Valley Forge with the skills that made him one of the most useful of all Washington's officers.

During that long, cold winter and into the spring, he drilled the American troops until the rankest amateurs had evolved into a cohesive, professional army. Drill became the main amusement of the camp as divisions tried to outdo one another, provoking hoots and catcalls, boasts and strutting, bets and challenges. Steuben's training did wonders for the formerly bored and dispirited soldiers. It was here that Joseph Bloomfield learned how to be a professional soldier.

On May 10, 1778 wonderful, long-awaited news arrived at Valley Forge. France had recognized the infant United States and become her ally; the treaty had been signed in February, followed by Spain and Holland, threatening the British naval supply route to Philadelphia. From now on, the war would become a different animal.

The British response to the news could not have been more gratifying: the gnashing of imperial teeth, impotent waving of imperial sabers, and the decision to withdraw from Philadelphia. General William Howe's resignation was accepted, and he sailed for home, leaving Sir Henry Clinton as British commander, the third so far during the three years of the war, with orders to take the British back to New York.

On the night of June 17, the troops and heavy field guns, heavy baggage, American refugees with their chattels were loaded on transports and ferried across to the Jersey shore from Philadelphia, where a baggage train was waiting for them to travel the road to Allentown. The full tide of war was sweeping into New Jersey again. The enormous train of vehicles—baggage and provision wagons, bakeries and blacksmith shops on wheels, a pontoon train, and the numerous private carriages of refugees—sometimes stretched out for eight or ten miles. Washington's army and state militiamen harried the retreating British for every mile they marched across New Jersey. It was a bitter pill for New Jersey Tories to swallow.

Evacuating Philadelphia, Clinton chose to march his 20,000 troops across New Jersey following a route that led from Cooper's Ferry (now Camden), to Mt. Holly and on to Allentown before arriving at Monmouth Court House (present day Freehold). At Allentown the road divided and Clinton decided to take the longer route to Sandy Hook, where he could board his army on ships for the final leg of the journey to New York. This would enable him to

Sir Henry Clinton, British Commander in Chief during the American Revolution. *Painting attributed to Andrea Soldi. American Museum in Britain.*

avoid crossing the Raritan River at New Brunswick with the huge unwieldy train, and also allow him to move away from the advancing American army that had crossed the Delaware at Lambertville.

All during the British move across New Jersey Americans skirmished with the British. On the morning of June 25, struggling over sandy roads in increasing heat, the tempo of American harassing attacks increased, and a combined Continental and militia force under New Jersey Continental Major Joseph Bloomfield hung within a quarter mile of the British rear, closing with and firing on the enemy "several times during the night." Bloomfield's detachment "took 15 prisoners had several skirmishes with the jaegers," with Major Bloomfield personally claiming three Jaeger prisoners.

On Sunday, June 28, 1778, a brutally hot and humid day, with temperatures soaring close to 100 degrees the Battle of Monmouth occurred. The hardest fought engagement of the American Revolution, it was also the longest day of all the British-American wars. It was a "pell-mell" contest between regiments and detachments, as opposed to brigades and divisions. General Charles Lee, who had been recently released in a prisoner exchange by the British after his incarceration from December 1776 to May 1778, added further confusion.

Considering an American victory unlikely, Lee favored a negotiated peace, and may have been influenced by his soft treatment while a captive. Overcome by Clinton's superior forces, Lee was forced to retreat, causing Washington to conclude Lee had not obeyed his orders to attack. Washington met the retreating forces and assumed command, desperately seeking to reorganize them.

Lee was blasphemous, rude, and unbearably slovenly in a day when cleanliness was not one of the cardinal virtues, and was followed everywhere by his pack of snapping dogs. All of his faults had previously been justified by his presumed bravery and military skill, but when Washington came up, he rallied the fleeing soldiers and loosed a rare titanic blast of rage at Lee.

Lee was the eccentric officer who had been a constant problem to General Washington. There was no question of his bravery and ability, but he refused

Charles Lee. *Engraving by Christoph Heinrich Korn. Library of Congress.*

to follow the instructions of his Commander in Chief. As a result, the Battle of Monmouth was not a complete victory.

When General Lee later died, the following provision was found in his will: "I desire most earnestly that I may not be buried in any church or churchyard, or within a mile of any Presbyterian or Anabaptist meetinghouse; for since I have resided in this country, (Lee was born in England) I have kept so much bad company when living, that I do not choose to continue it when dead."

The actions on the battlefield that day of Washington's second-in-command, General Lee, were considered by some of Washington's staff as reprehensible. Major Joseph Bloomfield wrote in his journal that the Continentals "drove the proud King's Guards & haughty British-Grenadiers, & gained Immortal-honor, to the Shame and infamy of General Lee."

More or less a draw, Monmouth was nevertheless heartening to the American public. The British suffered far greater casualties than the Americans:

"Washington at the Battle of Monmouth" *Painting by Emanuel Leutze (1816-1868). Oil on canvas, dated 1857. Monmouth County Historical Association, Freehold, New Jersey. Gift of the descendants of David Leavitt, 1937.*

Clinton suffered 1,200 casualties, including those wounded, killed, and captured, to Washington's 300-400.

That night, stretched on their cloaks on the ground, Washington and Lafayette discussed Lee's conduct until they eventually fell asleep. Not until dawn did they or anyone else in the American army learn that the British had stolen away in the midnight darkness and were far down the road toward Middletown, to be overtaken before they could rejoin the rest of their army. Lee was court martialed, found guilty for his insubordination and suspended from command; he left the army, along with his dogs—to the relief of all concerned.

Nathanael Greene. *Original portrait painted from life in 1783 by Charles Willson Peale.*

Monmouth provided solid evidence that the Americans had indeed finally created a regular army out of a force that had taken its first solid steps toward that goal during the winter and spring forage wars of 1777 in Middlesex, Essex and Somerset Counties. The day after the battle the New Jersey militia, their time now expired, marched home. Joseph Bloomfield resigned his commission, thus ending his Revolutionary War service. He had had enough of the war, and he proceeded to march home to Burlington to assume his duties as the newly elected clerk of the New Jersey Assembly.

The Battle of Monmouth, the hardest fought battle of the American Revolutionary War, was a political and psychological triumph for the Continental Army and for Washington, and marked a turning point in the conflict. By confining the British army in New York City for two more years, thus annihilating resistance, Washington had once again thwarted the British hope to win a quick victory.

From 1780 to 1781, Britain focused on the American South, a campaign that Nathanael Greene won using Washingtonian tactics, fighting six battles and losing five, but ultimately driving the British to Yorktown, where Washington commanded the final victory.

LIFE IN BURLINGTON

After retiring from army life on October 29, 1778, Joseph Bloomfield soon married Mary McIlvaine. The couple settled in Burlington in a circa 1750 mansion "with a fine library and many curiosities," and he resumed the practice of law. The Bloomfields had no children, but adopted and raised their nephew Joseph McIlvaine. Bloomfield's political and official life dates from his resignation from the army.

On October 28, 1778, he was elected clerk of the New Jersey Assembly, and from 1779 to 1783 he served as register of the Court of Admiralty. He served as president of the first Society for the Abolition of Slavery, organized in Burlington in 1783, and hosted meetings of that organization in his home. In 1783 he became attorney general of the State, resigning from that office in 1792. He served as a trustee for the College of New Jersey at Princeton from 1793 to 1801.

As presidential elector in 1792, he voted for Washington and Adams, but after developing a friendly acquaintance with Thomas Jefferson soon thereafter, he became a prominent leader of the Republicans in New Jersey. From 1795 to 1800 he was the mayor of Burlington. After a period of indecision, Bloomfield emerged as one of the few genuine landed aristocrats in New Jersey to join the Jeffersonian cause, as opposed to the more mainline Federalist Party, in the decade following the ratification of the Federal Constitution in June, 1788.

The state's largest county, at over eight hundred square miles, Burlington was even larger when New Jersey was a British colony and it dominated West Jersey. It included portions of today's Hunterdon, Mercer, Morris, Ocean, Sussex, and Warren Counties. The county seat, Burlington City, was prosperous and had a number of Loyalists during the Revolution, including

James Fenimore Cooper. *Photo by Mathew Brady, 1850*

Royal Governor William Franklin from 1763 to 1774, the mayor of Burlington, John Lawrence, and the Rector of St. Mary's Anglican Church, Jonathan Odell, who used his pulpit to promote Loyalists. Vocal Patriots such as Francis Hopkinson, a signer of the Declaration of Independence, made it

James Lawrence. *Painting by J. Herring, after Gilbert Stuart. Naval History & Heritage Command, United States Navy.*

clear that those loyal to the crown risked incarceration, and in fact Lawrence was jailed and Franklin and Odell left America for England.

Burlington was also the birthplace of James Fenimore Cooper, and his home still stands beside that of Captain James Lawrence. Cooper, the well-known author of *The Leatherstocking Tales*, which included "The Last of the

Mohicans" and "The Deerslayer," was born in Burlington in 1789 and later moved with his parents to Cooperstown, New York. Cooper served in the U.S. Navy from 1808 to 1811, and published his first book in 1820

The residence of Joseph Bloomfield in Burlington, on the corner of Main and Library Streets, is a three-story brick structure with a mansard roof. It was previously the home of Elizabeth Lawrence. She married Michael Kearny and made their home at the Kearny Cottage, Perth Amboy, now a city-owned historic site. Elizabeth's half-brother, Capt. James Lawrence of "Don't give up the ship" fame, moved with her from Burlington to Perth Amboy as a young boy after his parents died. There Lawrence would watch the ships arriving in the port of Perth Amboy with goods as far away as India and dream of someday going to sea.

POST REVOLUTION

The Articles of Confederation and The United Stated Constitution

George Washington issued a cease-fire on April 9, 1783, and by April 15 Congress had proclaimed the war's end. Soon discovering that it was easier to defeat tyranny than to establish popular government, he wrote to Lafayette in April, 1783 "We are placed among the nations of the earth and have a character to establish…the probability, at least I fear it is, that local or state politics will interfere too much with that more liberal and extensive plan of government which wisdom and foresight, freed from the midst of prejudice, would dictate."

During the war Washington had compared America's political system to a clock, vulnerable to sudden breakdown if the smaller wheels were maintained at the expense of the larger ones. In a similar vein, while retired at Mount Vernon he railed against the unreasonable demands of individual states and the importance of the central government. "This is as clear to me as the A, B, C; and I think we have opposed Great Britain….to very little purpose if we can not conquer our own prejudices," he contended. He embraced an energetic government as the only means of protecting the American union against its centrifugal tendencies.

In December 1783 the New Jersey Legislature declared that until Congress was vested with the power to collect tariff duties, it would make no further contributions to support the Articles of Confederation. In February of 1786, New Jersey again reaffirmed this position. The state equally insisted, since it had no claim to any western lands, that these tracts should belong to the states collectively as an important source of revenue for the central government.

New Jersey contended that the region west of the Appalachian Mountains belonged rightfully to the nation as a whole rather than those states like Virginia, New York and North Carolina that laid claim to huge areas based

The Constitution of the United States of America.

on their early charters. New Jersey citizens felt that if they were under the control of Congress, the people of New Jersey would have equal access to them.

Ultimately the cessions were made, and Congress arranged for the disposal of its vast domain by sales to individuals and speculative companies. In New Jersey a group of enterprising men headed by John Cleves Symmes, and including such notaries as Elias Boudinot, Jonathan Dayton, General Elias Dayton, and Joseph Bloomfield, entered into negotiations with Congress in 1787 and purchased an expansive tract in southwestern Ohio along the Great Miami River. This led to the founding of the city of Cincinnati (originally Losantville) and the naming of the city of Dayton.

By 1787, in post-American Revolutionary War New Jersey, some degree of order had been instituted to pay for the state's debts and the major tasks of rehabilitation and reconstruction had been accomplished. But not all was in perfect order. New Jersey's relations with the central government were unsatisfactory, and indeed, its confidence in that government was negligible. What was needed was a new frame of government to replace the Articles of Confederation.

Preceded only by Delaware and Pennsylvania, the Federal Constitution was unanimously ratified on December 17, 1787 by the convention of New Jersey, meeting in Perth Amboy. Chief Justice John Marshall, who had served with General Mercer's Flying Camp in Perth Amboy in 1776, insisted that among the Founding Fathers, none supported the Constitution more than Alexander Hamilton, who had done so much to see it approved by each state. James Madison expressed his approval by writing that the government of the United States was "the best legacy ever left by lawgivers to their country and the best lesson ever given to the world."

CROSS KEYS TAVERN

*George Washington's Visit and Inauguration as
First President of the United States*

Politicking stopped temporarily in April 1789, when George Washington passed through New Jersey on his way to New York to be sworn in as first president of the United States. On April 16, 1789, he and his entourage had left his home at Mount Vernon, Virginia, and headed north. It took them a full week to cover the 250-mile journey to New York City, the nation's first capital.

The party's plan was to be on the road by 5:30 a.m., with travel taking place throughout the remainder of the day. But at every stop along the route—Baltimore, Wilmington, Philadelphia, Trenton, Princeton, New Brunswick and Woodbridge—there were welcoming delegations and honor guards that flanked Washington's coach, official receptions and banquets to attend, and speeches and toasts that required a response. Cannons boomed, bells rang, and bridges were draped with magnificent wreaths.

George Washington's New Jersey campaigns had been crucial to the development of his national reputation. The state, in effect, had become a second home to Washington, as he had fought more battles on its soil than anywhere else during the eight long years of the war. Washington had spent more time in New Jersey than in any other state, and it would remain a special place in his memory. The general would never forget the "Jerseys," nor would the Jersey people ever forget him.

Many historians call the Battle of Trenton the most important battle in American history. While addressing the New Jersey General Assembly at Trenton on December 6, 1783, Washington spoke of the people of the state who, after being overrun by the enemy, had rallied and driven the invader from their home.

Congress had chosen George Washington as their Commander of the Continental Army. This was a rare tribute—that the men from New England had turned to a man from Virginia to be their leader. After all, they were a region known for their sympathy with resistance and revolution, and their fiery outspokenness. The soldierly qualities of the man from the South, his gift for leadership, and his personal distinction could not be ignored, and the North was ready to follow his trail.

Unswerving in his leadership since Cambridge, where he took his command and ousted the British from Boston forever, then continuing as he crossed New Jersey, a region strong in adversity, his military genius and triumphs that followed at Trenton and Princeton gave uplift to the army and to Congress. At Monmouth, stirred to vehemence by treachery in the ranks, he finished in a victory over the perfidy of General Charles Lee. Now passing through "the Jarseys" in April 1789, Washington remembered the warm reception that he had been given at the Indian Queen Tavern in New Brunswick after he had said a final goodbye to his officers at Fraunces Tavern in New York City on December 4, 1783, before proceeding on to Trenton and later Mount Vernon.

Traveling once more across the Jersey Midlands, he may have been recalling the major role William Paterson (later the first of New Jersey's two senators, second governor of New Jersey and associate justice of the United States Supreme Court) and New Jersey had played in the development of the new United States Constitution on June 15, 1787. Paterson had been instrumental in New Jersey's leading the way to the United States bicameral system of government which we enjoy today.

And so it was that "an admiring concourse" greeted Washington, the president-elect, as he entered Trenton on April 21, 1789. This event was memorialized in a Nathanael Currier lithograph depicting the general and his party passing under a flower-festooned archway, visibly touched by the message on the arch:

DONALD JOHNSTONE PECK

THE DEFENDER OF THE MOTHERS WILL BE THE PROTECTOR OF THE DAUGHTERS

White-robed young girls and thirteen young women (each representing a state) strewed flowers in Washington's path as they sang an ode written especially for the occasion by Major Richard Howell (later Governor Howell, the third governor of New Jersey (1793-1801):

> Welcome, mighty Chief! Once more
> Welcome to this grateful shore!
> Now no mercenary foe
> Aims again the fatal blow-
> Aims at thee the fatal blow.
>
> Virgins fair and matrons grave,
> These thy conquering arms did save,
> Build for thee triumphal bowers,
> Strew, ye fair, his way with flowers,
> Strew our hero's way with flowers

Washington thanked Trenton's "matrons and young ladies" who received him "in so novel and grateful a manner at the Triumphal Arch in Trenton" and moved on to stay overnight in Princeton. Along the way "farmers assembled at crossroads, gentry bowed dignified welcome from the porches of wayside inns, and soldiers who had fought their nation's battles saluted and cheered."

Departing New Brunswick on Sunday, April 22, Washington's entourage proceeded on the King's Highway (present day Woodbridge Avenue, Route 514 East) to St. James Episcopal Church, Piscataway (now Edison Township) for a Service of Morning Prayer. They then continued east through Bonhamtown, crossing Poplar Hill and Fords (present day Upper Main Street). Continuing on they then crossed over Heard's Brook, as it gurgled below them, and entered the town of Woodbridge. The cheers of the local citizenry enveloped Washington's party as the people sang the tune "Yankee Doodle" to them.

George Washington's triumphant entrance into Trenton was celebrated in this lithograph by Nathanael Currier. *Author's collection.*

Accompanied by Charles Thompson, Colonel Humphreys, and his mulatto body servant, Billy Lee, the celebrated visitor and his company were escorted to the Cross Keys Tavern by the Woodbridge Cavalry, commanded by Captain Ichabod Potter, where they stayed the night. The innkeeper at the time was John Manning. Here Washington was given a tumultuous reception by a large military and civilian contingent, including the first New Jersey State Governor, William Livingston of Liberty Hall, Elizabethtown.

The Cross Keys Tavern had been a cradle of revolt. It was the headquarters for revolution in Woodbridge and a popular rallying place for the Sons of Liberty to discuss their grievances. This was the gathering spot where colonists had criticized their king, merchants had voiced protest over harsh British trade restrictions, travelers had brought news of similar ferment in other colonies, petitions were drawn up and signed, tea boycotts were organized, and militia units had been formed.

The Cross Keys Tavern. *Painting by Francis McGinley. Author's collection.*

The Commander-in-Chief had chosen local taverns for his headquarters on many occasions. During the winter of 1777 he stayed at the Jacob Arnold Tavern in Morristown. Many taverns had been burned, particularly by Loyalist forces wreaking their revenge on innkeepers, some of whom were former friends known to be supporting the American cause. As the oldest and most important historic building still standing in Woodbridge Township, it is most fortunate that, although modified, this celebrated historic site is still extant.

The Cross Keys Tavern has become a lost American treasure, as have so many other fine buildings of our historical and cultural past, which have been neglected, forgotten or destroyed. Moved one block north to Upper James Street in the early 1920s, it still stands virtually unnoticed today, its former prominent location now replaced with a Knights of Columbus clubhouse.

The *cross keys* refer to the key roads leading to somewhere important. In this case, the key roads were the King's Highway, which led north to Newark and south to the provincial and state capital, Perth Amboy, and the Old Dutch Road or Upper Road (Route 514) that led from Elizabethtown Point to Woodbridge and then to New Brunswick, Princeton, and Trenton.

Lost to time is the celebrated Elm Tree Tavern, famous for its giant Elm tree, which stood nearby in the old historic district of Woodbridge on Rahway Avenue, and the Pike Tavern at Heard's Square at the foot of Green Street, which hosted Benjamin Franklin when he visited James Parker. Also no longer standing is the Widow White's Tavern, Basking Ridge, where the British captured Washington's second-in-command, General Charles Lee, on December 15, 1776.

Fortunately still standing and restored are the Englishtown Tavern (where Charles Lee's court martial first took place after the Battle of Monmouth), the refurbished Indian Queen Tavern of New Brunswick (now relocated and reconstructed in East Jersey Olde Towne Village, Piscataway) and the Indian King Tavern of Haddonfield.

Lined up to greet Washington along his route were many of the surviving Woodbridge residents who had taken part in the struggle for independence during the twenty-nine skirmishes that occurred in the Woodbridge area. Among the notables were Brigadier General Nathaniel Heard (then Colonel Heard) who commanded the Middlesex County Militia, and who had arrested Royal Governor William Franklin on June 19, 1776 at the Proprietary House in Perth Amboy. As mentioned earlier, the Provincial Congress, of which Moses Bloomfield was one of the five deputies elected from Middlesex County, issued the arrest order.

Washington surely reminisced about how in mid-January, 1776 the Continental Congress had sent Colonel Heard with 1,200 militia to suppress the Tories of Queens County, New York. Using a voter list, Heard's militia scoured the county for two weeks and administered a test oath to 800 Loyalists. In addition, he confiscated 1,000 muskets and arrested nineteen of the twenty-six most active Tory leaders.

Also in attendance on that day in April was Major Zebulon Montgomery Pike, a descendant of John Pike, one of the original settlers of Woodbridge. Pike, of War of 1812 fame, discovered 14,110-foot-high Pike's Peak in the Rocky Mountains, near Colorado Springs, Colorado, in 1806. His aunt, Janet Pike Gage, was said to have raised a Liberty Pole to fly the Stars and Stripes for the first time at the local Cross Keys Tavern.

Many other residents of Woodbridge who had served as officers in the Continental Army were also present. They included Colonel Samuel Crow, General Clarkson Edgar, Captain David Edgar, Colonel Benjamin Brown and Lieutenant James Paten. Remembered were Captains Nathaniel Fitz Randolph, who lost his life in the last battle to be fought in the north, the Second Battle of Springfield on June 23, 1780, and David Edgar, Matthew Sayers, Ellis Barron and Abraham Tappen, all of whom now quietly rest in the Old Burying Ground of the First Presbyterian Church.

George Washington reflected deeply about the last British invasion of New Jersey, which occurred on June 6, 1780 and came to a climax on June 23. In his full-length study of the Battle of Springfield, Thomas Fleming, author of *The Forgotten Victory*, pointed out that there were sound military

Wilhelm von Knyphausen. *Print Collection, Miriam and Ira D. Wallach Division of Art, Humanities and Social Sciences Library, NY*

reasons why the Battle of Springfield was fought. Hessian Lieutenant General Baron Wilhelm von Knyphausen, anxious to strike, believed that the Americans were demoralized. But the shrewd delaying tactics of Quartermaster General Nathanael Greene caused von Knyphausen and his battleground staff to retreat over the Arthur Kill and back to Staten Island. This is one reason that Washington considered Greene the best of his generals, suitable to succeed him in case of death or capture.

The Reverend Dr. Azel Roe, pastor of the Old White Church (the First Presbyterian Church), was honored to also be in attendance. He had preached the religious legitimating of independence from his pulpit, as had Rev. John Witherspoon in Princeton. A Scottish-born Presbyterian, Dr. Roe had no love for the English. He had taken part in one of the skirmishes at Blazing Star (now Carteret), and was captured by the British and imprisoned for a time at the notorious Old Sugar House prison in New York City.

Also present was prominent Woodbridge resident Dr. Moses Bloomfield, who had freed his slaves on July 4, 1783. Unlike Moses Bloomfield's position on slave holding, George Washington's interest in victory led him down some unfamiliar paths. Within months of taking command, the Virginia slave-owner agreed to let free Negroes remain in his army on the grounds that to expel them would only spur British recruitment.

A later visitor to the Cross Keys Tavern, but missing on this particular day, was the Marquis de Lafayette. Without the French involvement in the War for Independence, the American cause surely would not have been successful. Shortly after the French Alliance with the United States in 1778 Washington had thanked "the Almighty ruler of the Universe" for the French Alliance. There was no Frenchman, indeed no man, whom he loved more than Lafayette.

This mural depicts the arrival of Reverend Roe in 1804. *Mural by Lloyd Garrison, 1968. First Presbyterian Church of Woodbridge Township.*

Rev. Azel Roe. *First Presbyterian Church of Woodbridge Township.*

In July of 1777, the nineteen-year-old French nobleman had arrived at American headquarters. Fired with a desire for glory and fed up with a miserable life ruled by his overbearing father-in-law, the Marquis de Lafayette had broken free and sailed to America, hoping to learn from General Washington. Impressed by his position and wealth, Congress appointed him a major general of the Continental Army—even though he had no military experience whatsoever.

Left childless by nature, Washington was paternal by instinct. The general treated Lafayette as a son, while the young man, in ardent yet fractured English, regarded Washington as "the salvation of his country and the admiration of the universe." If George Washington had a surrogate son, it was this red-haired Frenchman of noble birth and liberal politics.

Many years later, on September 24, 1824, the illustrious Marquis de Lafayette, "the hero of two worlds," visited Woodbridge and was given elaborate ceremonies on the town green near the intersection of Rahway Avenue and Freeman Street. During his visit Lafayette stayed at the Cross

Gilbert du Motier Marquis de Lafayette. *Painting by Joseph-Désiré Court.*

Elias Boudinot. *Painting by Thomas Sully.*

Keys Tavern. In the course of his subsequent travels across the United States, he was received with celebrations, processions, dinners, bonfires, and balls from the moment he returned to America until the day he left for France.

At Woodbridge one of the special features of his reception was the presence of sixteen little girls dressed in white, each bearing on her dress a letter made of marigolds, which together formed the words "Welcome Lafayette." A large choir composed of Woodbridge school children and others also entertained the general with patriotic songs.

On the morning of April 23, 1789, Washington left Woodbridge and traveled to Rahway, where military companies from Newark, Connecticut Farms and Elizabethtown escorted him to Boxwood Hall in the latter city. This substantial house was the residence of Elias Boudinot, president of the Continental Congress from 1782 to 1783, and here Boudinot entertained the president-elect. Washington then departed from Elizabethtown Point and boarded an "elegantly adorned" crimson-canopied, forty-seven-foot barge, propelled by uniformed oarsmen. The vessel carried him past a flotilla of wildly cheering crowds in colorfully bedecked small craft across Newark and Lower New York Bay. He landed to a stupendous ovation at lower Manhattan, where he was inaugurated on April 30. "All ranks

James Madison. *Painting by John Vanderlyn. The White House Historical Association.*

and professions," ran one newspaper account, "expressed their feelings in loud acclamations, and with rapture hailed the arrival of the Father of His Country."

History records Washington's earliest biographer, David Humphreys, as perhaps a better psychologist than author. Being rowed across New York Harbor toward his inauguration, Humphreys later wrote, Washington was "filled with sensations as painful as they were pleasing." He took the oath of office on the balcony of Federal Hall before an estimated crowd of 10,000, or nearly one third of cheering New Yorkers, telling them, "I was summoned by my country, whose voice I can never hear but with veneration and love." And so the Virginia planter-turned-soldier-turned-chief-executive forsook his rural seat on the Potomac for the crowded streets and tangled intrigues of Manhattan, a city of about 30,000 people at the time.

As their hero journeyed to New York the wishful thinking that Trenton might become the nation's capitol lingered in the back of the minds of many onlookers. This idea had been floated about in Congress as early as 1783. Although Washington, D.C. would later become our nation's capitol, on November 25, 1790 the New Jersey State Legislature chose Trenton as the permanent seat of state government despite opposition from New Brunswick and Woodbury.

The state's first governor, William Livingston, would miss the decision to move the capitol to Trenton. In his fourteenth year as governor of the state, he died in Elizabethtown on July 25, 1790. He had been the chief executive through war and peace, and his standards of personal conduct and his ability to realize the power of his office have rarely been matched.

Washington's first year in office was surprisingly uneventful, in keeping with the new president's wishes. Prodded on by James Madison, who labeled it a "nauseous project" marked by incessant posturing and verbal warfare, Congress adopted twelve amendments to the Constitution, of which ten were subsequently consented to by the states to form the Bill of Rights. New Jersey was the first state to ratify them on November 20, 1789, in the present-day City Hall in Perth Amboy.

FEDERALIST VERSUS REPUBLICAN

A Two Party System

Joseph Bloomfield was named chairman of the first statewide Democratic-Republican nominating convention, a party device introduced to cultivate unity for the pending congressional and presidential elections; he emerged as the titular leader of the party. The citizens of Burlington County gathered in Springfield Township on September 20, 1800, to endorse the national ticket, appoint committees of correspondence, and plan future Democratic-Republican activity in New Jersey. Joseph Bloomfield chaired the meeting. It should be kept in mind that today's Republican Party was not formed until 1854.

In a fiery speech typical of the period, Bloomfield urged that the New Jersey Constitution not be revised and that wealthy federalist speculators not be permitted to taint American democracy. His speech contained a two-page statement of incriminating evidence against Federalist spending and rampant speculation and ended with the universal question: "Is it not high time for a change?" His strong endorsement of Democratic-Republican candidates was followed by an address from Stephen Sayre, Secretary of the Republican Citizens of Burlington County.

Although the Democratic-Republicans were unsuccessful in carrying New Jersey for Thomas Jefferson and Aaron Burr in the election of 1800, they developed new forms of organizing and soliciting the support of voters for their cause. This intensive organizing was based on county committees of correspondence campaigning independently, and later collating their efforts through popular organs such as party newspapers and pamphlets.

THE PRESS

At the outbreak of the Revolution, the population of New Jersey looked to nine Pennsylvania papers—three of which were printed in German—and to their four contemporaries in New York City. In 1751 James Parker established the first press in New Jersey in Woodbridge. His periodical, the *American Magazine*, on sale seven years later, succumbed after two years because of lack of patronage. Isaac Collins printed the state's first newspaper, the *New Jersey Gazette*, on December 5, 1767, at Burlington, New Jersey, but discontinued it by 1768. By 1787 there were four more.

The heat of partisanship during the Revolution had led to the rise of a local press including the *Elizabeth Daily Journal*. The passionate controversy between Hamilton's Federalism and Jefferson's Republicanism gave way to new opinionated papers, including the ardent Federalist advocate, the *Newark Gazette*, in 1791, and the equally vehement tabloid for states' rights, Morristown's *Sentinel of Freedom*, founded in 1796.

With the death William Livingston, New Jersey's first governor after independence, the legislature chose William Paterson of Raritan (Somerville) to succeed him. An early backer of independence, Paterson had served well in the Constitutional Convention as a warm champion of states' rights. Calling for each state to have equal representation regardless of size, he said "New Jersey would not have sent delegates to any assembly that would destroy the equalities and rights of the state." In 1790, when the first U. S. Census was taken, New Jersey's population was about 185,000 people.

William Paterson, as both a promoter of state's rights and a bi-cameral form of government, played a significant role at the Constitutional Convention, where he is best remembered for the *New Jersey Plan*, which called for two senators from each state. This plan provided for federal supremacy, equal representation in the Senate, a federal judiciary, the *Three Fifths* clause (giving southern states partial representation in Congress for slaves), and the *commerce clause*—giving jurisdiction over interstate commerce to the federal government.

Paterson became one of New Jersey's first two senators, the other being Jonathan Elmer of Cumberland County. Elmer's brother, Ebenezer, had

William Paterson. *Painting by C. Gregory Stapko, copied from James Sharples.*

been one of the seven arsonists acquitted by Joseph Bloomfield at the trial of the Greenwich Tea Party back in April, 1775. Paterson soon became a leading Federalist, urging support for a strong national government. When he accepted George Washington's appointment to the United States Supreme Court in 1793, another champion of strong federal power, William Howell of Trenton, succeeded him as governor.

The Federalists rode high in New Jersey and elsewhere in the decade after the adoption of the Constitution. Chief national spokesman of the Federalist cause was Alexander Hamilton, Washington's brilliant, caustic young Secretary of the Treasury. The Federalist program combined a strong central government with a unified financial structure, topped by a presidential cult of personality bordering on adulation.

Although there was as of yet no formally organized opposition party, neither was there any shortage of anti-Federalists, whose earlier suspicions of the Constitution were daily confirmed by Hamilton's seeming disregard for states' rights, agrarian interests, and the classical Republican antipathy toward concentrated power.

Hamilton's career touched New Jersey intimately during the period of Federalist supremacy. It was he who proposed creating an industrial town for manufacturing at the 70-foot Great Falls of the Passaic River for his "Society for Establishing Useful Manufactures." The site of Paterson, like that of Washington, D.C., was deliberately chosen for a purpose, and it started as America's first planned industrial city in 1792. Major L'Enfant, the French engineer who designed the plan of the national capital, was asked to chart its power canals, mills and residential districts.

The declining Federalist power within New Jersey had been well underway with the election of Thomas Jefferson in 1800, with their idea that the power of a nation must rest within the hands of "the people" rather than in an aristocracy. In 1801 Joseph Bloomfield was elected New Jersey's first anti-Federalist governor, a post he held until 1812.

The debut of the new party politics also brought about substantial changes in the media. The two brand-new parties, Democratic-Republican and Federalist, now purchased controlling interests in the weekly newspapers in different cities and used them to launch scurrilous attacks on their opponents and their leaders.

Alexander Hamilton. *Library of Congress.*

In a speech that Alexander Hamilton made on June 18, 1787 during the Federal Constitutional Convention in Philadelphia, as recorded by James Madison, Hamilton, referring to notes for this speech, revealed his preferences:

"British constitution best form…
Two political divisions—the few and the many…
They should be separated…
If separated, they will need a mutual check.
This check is a monarch…
There ought to be a principle in government capable of resisting the popular current…
The monarch…ought to be hereditary, and have so much power that it will not be in his interest to risk much to acquire more"

During Washington's first term, Hamilton grew into a devoted nationalist, determined to expand the powers of the federal government and to convince the states to see the benefit of a strong union. Jefferson was just the opposite, determined to lessen the national government's grip on the public and the states. "The natural progress of things is for liberty to yield and government to gain ground," warned Jefferson, who, with Madison, started the Jeffersonian Republican political party, a well-organized group that eventually gave birth to America's two party system.

PHILIP FRENEAU

Undoubtedly the fiercest anti-Federalist was Philip Freneau, a former college roommate of James Madison at Princeton. After they graduated, the colonies were still fiercely loyal to the king. Freneau had shocked the school at the commencement exercises by lauding the Boston Massacre. He was, in his way, as colorful as almost any of the outstanding figures New Jersey has given to the nation.

"Poet of the Revolution" and "Father of American Poetry," Freneau was hailed by Thomas Jefferson as savior of our Constitution when the country was "galloping fast into monarchy." Known today mainly as a writer of verse and of prose which was often violently political and patriotic in tone, Freneau was a busy merchant and sea captain who made many voyages to southern ports, the West Indies, and the island of Madeira for wine cargoes.

Philip Morin Freneau, a contemporary of Joseph Bloomfield, was born in 1752. As was Joseph Bloomfield, Freneau was witness to and participant

Philip Freneau. *Engraving by Frederick Halpin.*

in many historic events through the Revolutionary crisis: the writing and adoption of the Constitution, the Federalist era, the Jeffersonian "revolution," the War of 1812, and the Era of Good Feelings. According to author Thomas

D. Cowan, it cannot be stated too strongly that Freneau hated Federalism and all its works and pomps.

Numerous poems, essays, and articles attest to Freneau's driving crusade to spread Jeffersonian Republicanism and defeat the forces of Federalism. Jefferson's well-known remark that it was primarily Freneau who saved the republic from "galloping into monarchy" during Washington's administration attests to the poet's role in the early political feuds between the Jeffersonians and Hamiltonians.

Washington was extremely sensitive to hostile criticism. Though he attracted it less than any other president, he did receive some, chiefly from a handful of republican editors who called him variously a gambler, a cheapskate, a horse beater, a dictator, and "a most horrid swearer and blasphemer." Jefferson knew full well that Washington was complaining of the tone of Philip Freneau's *National Gazette*.

Freneau voiced Republican ideas that detested and vilified every form of monarchy or aristocracy, which he believed subversive to the true national character. He accused the country of rampant commercialism and unscrupulous merchants and feared the survival of the republic because of commerce. "Ready access to the luxuries of life leads merchants to sensuality and indulgence," he said. "Too much commercialism leads to luxuries which in turn lead to aristocracy."

During the Revolution, Freneau joined the Monmouth militia, patrolling the coast as "scout and guard" with his dog Sancho. Shipping on a vessel trying to run the British blockade, he was captured and languished in a prison ship, an experience that deeply influenced his writing and thinking. In 1791 Jefferson, now Secretary of State, named him to a "clerkship in foreign languages" at a salary of $250 per year, in Philadelphia. It was there that Freneau founded the influential *National Gazette*. Through its columns, Freneau plunged into the bitter Jefferson-Hamilton feud, militantly backing Jefferson.

He so persistently urged American support of the French Revolution that Washington denounced him at a cabinet meeting as "that rascal Freneau" for embarrassing the administration, while Jefferson saluted him as champion of the common man. Freneau, a residential section of the town of Matawan,

The grave of Philip Freneau. *Photo courtesy Gordon Bond.*

Marker at the site of the Freneau grave. *Photo courtesy Gordon Bond.*

New Jersey, was named for Philip Freneau. Here at Freneau Farm, he had published his *New Jersey Chronicle.* His nearby grave is marked with a marble shaft.

As with Thomas Paine, to Federalists Freneau appeared as a misfit in his day. According to Cowan, Jeffersonian Republicanism, love of France and respect for Thomas Paine were as subversive and "un-American" as was Communism in the Twentieth Century.

For the next twenty-five years, from the time of the signing of the Treaty of Paris in 1783 ending the American Revolution, Jefferson, Madison and the men they encountered in Philadelphia and New York would battle over the two highest offices in the land. In 1796 John Adams and Jefferson opposed each other for the presidency, with Adams winning and Jefferson becoming Vice President. Four years later Jefferson won the rematch, but only because Hamilton supported him over his running mate, Aaron Burr, Jr.

After the war, Burr, as a civilian and lawyer in New York City, plunged into the presidential campaign of 1800 to help elect Jefferson, and handled the Tammany Organization so skillfully that the ticket won, with Burr astonishingly tied in electoral votes with Jefferson. Congress broke the tie, as was the custom, and Burr became vice president as a result of Hamilton maneuvered things for Jefferson behind the scenes.

Hamilton schemed to keep Aaron Burr, Jr. from being named president in 1800. In 1804 Hamilton frustrated Burr's ambition to be elected governor of New York. Hamilton backed Charles Pinckney over President John Adams in the election of 1800, with Thomas Jefferson and Aaron **B**urr, Jr.

also running. Hamilton wrote a scathing denunciation of Adams that was intended only for the eyes of certain party leaders, but Burr published it as a public document and it created a political firestorm.

The Electoral College could not pick a president, with Jefferson and Burr tied for first and John Adams for third. The election was thrown into the House of Representatives. Hamilton then abandoned Pinckney and urged the House to select his

Aaron Burr. *Painting by John Vanderlyn.*

archenemy, Jefferson, as president in order to get back at his enemy, Burr. The House elected Jefferson as president, and Burr and his supporters were understandably angered by Hamilton's actions.

Four years later, Hamilton worked against Burr when Burr ran for governor of New York. His successful opposition to Burr once again gained him many enemies. He wondered how he had begun his public life as the admired right-hand man of General Washington and wound up the center of so much criticism. He wrote near the end of his days that, "Mine is an odd destiny... this American world was not made for me."

BURR VERSUS HAMILTON

No doubt about it, the stormiest and most controversial figure New Jersey has contributed to the nation's history was Aaron Burr, Jr., born in Newark in 1756, another contemporary of Joseph Bloomfield. As young men, both Burr and Alexander Hamilton had attended the Old Academy on the grounds of the First Presbyterian Church in Elizabethtown. But after that their careers went in different directions—Hamilton became an aide to General George Washington during the war, and Burr managed to incur the lasting distrust of Washington himself.

This spotlight of fame and notoriety glared upon Burr most of his life. He moved as an equal among the great of the new country. He missed being elected president by one vote, and later slew in a duel the man mainly responsible for blocking him—Alexander Hamilton. Burr's father was president of the College of New Jersey (now Princeton University), his mother a daughter of the noted evangelist Jonathan Edwards. Burr's father, an evangelical preacher during New Jersey's *Great Awakening*, Aaron Burr, Sr. had helped found the College of New Jersey at Elizabethtown in 1746 for the training of ministers.

Burr had a brilliant military career throughout the Revolution. He enlisted as a private, saw service at Boston, and emerged from the Canadian Expedition a major. He spent the bitter winter of 1777-1778 at Valley Forge with Washington, and as a lieutenant colonel at the Battle of Monmouth in June 1778.

Furious that Hamilton's work had denied him both the presidency and the governorship, Burr challenged Hamilton to a duel. In the early morning of July 11, 1804, Hamilton climbed a Weehawken cliff of the Palisades, three

Illustration of the Hamilton - Burr duel. *Illustrator not identified. From a painting by J. Mund. - Lord, John, LL.D. (1902). Beacon Lights of History. Vol. XI, "American Founders." (London: James Clarke and Co Ltd.)*

hundred feet above the Hudson River in New Jersey, to a small grassy plain and there met his long-time political enemy. This was the same spot where Hamilton's son, Philip, had been killed in a duel three years earlier. Here Aaron Burr, then Vice President of the United States, mortally wounded Hamilton, the first Secretary of the Treasury.

The rendezvous had been in the making for many years. For fifteen years the two men had been political enemies, but it was not until Hamilton's libelous criticisms reached the press that Burr issued the challenge. The two men fired in succession at the command, "Present!" and Hamilton's bullet passed through the limb of a cedar tree about twelve feet above the ground, while Burr's shot caught his opponent in the breast. Hamilton died on the afternoon of the following day. Inflamed by the press to view Burr as a murderer, both New York and New Jersey indicted him.

On the evening of July 11, 1804 Burr fled to Perth Amboy to take refuge at "Pleasant View," the home of Commodore Thomas Truxton overlooking

Raritan Bay, and was entertained overnight there. Built by Royal Governor Robert Hunter in 1710, it had also been the residence of Royal Governor William Burnet. The next day, en route to Pennsylvania, according to local legend in Cranbury, New Jersey, Burr concealed himself at the home of Dr. Hezekiah Stites on South Main Street. This is the same house where Washington, Lafayette and Hamilton had met on June 26, 1778 before the Battle of Monmouth.

On August 2, 1804, the coroner's jury delivered the verdict Burr had dreaded. Aaron Burr, Esquire, Vice President of the United States, was guilty of the murder of Alexander Hamilton. An arrest warrant was issued. On August 14, before Burr learned that a New York grand jury had replaced the murder indictment with a lesser charge, Burr hid out on St. Simons Island, off the Georgia coast.

With threats of extradition, and outraged lynch mobs out to capture him, Burr then fled to the west on an expedition that remains an American mystery. He became involved in major land schemes and perhaps had planned to seize and found an empire in the Southwest or Mexico, where the dueling code was respected. He stayed there until Congress reconvened on November 4 and the temper of the country had cooled down. He had outlived his brief usefulness for the Republicans.

For much of his second term Jefferson tried to have Burr convicted of treason. Burr was acquitted for a lack of evidence. He died in 1836 and was buried at The Princeton Cemetery beside his distinguished educator father, Aaron Burr, Sr. John Adams was to have the last word when he left this epitaph of the man: "Burr's life, take it all together, was such as in any country of sound morals his friends would be desirous of burying in profound oblivion."

Weehawken's dueling ground provided melancholy punctuation for the chapter of declining Federal power in New Jersey. The trend had been well underway with the election of Thomas Jefferson and his position that the power of the nation must rest with "the people" rather than in the aristocracy. In 1808 James Madison was elected the fourth President of the United States, keeping Clinton on as Vice President, and Jefferson happily retired to Monticello. There he finally learned how to relax.

THE GOVERNORSHIP

The Gradual Emancipation Act of 1804

Joseph Bloomfield had been a key figure in cementing the Jefferson party organization in New Jersey during the years 1796-1800. After a period of indecision, Bloomfield emerged as one of the few genuine "landed aristocrats" in New Jersey to join the Jeffersonian cause instead of the more mainline Federalists Party in the decade following the ratification of the Federal Constitution. He continued to identify with Republican Party issues, opposing both the foreign policies of John Adams and the Alien and Sedition Acts of 1798.

The New Jersey Jeffersonian Party's efforts in these elections marked its coming of age, and in 1801, for the first time, it captured control of the state. Bloomfield's leadership was instrumental in achieving that victory, and the Jeffersonian legislative majority elected him governor for the constitutionally prescribed one-year term.

In 1802-03, because of a legislative deadlock (a tie for the office between Bloomfield and Richard Stockton IV), John Lambert, then vice president of Council, performed the duties of the governor's office. The next year Joseph Bloomfield received thirty-three votes and Richard Stockton seventeen, and in 1804, he had thirty-seven votes to his opponent's sixteen. Afterward, until 1812, he was reelected with awesome regularity.

Described by a contemporary as "rich," and taking great pride in his military service (he preferred to be called "General" rather than "Excellency"), Bloomfield managed to combine the roles of governor and party leader during his long tenure in office. He combined his personal authority with the prestige he commanded in Washington, D.C. as an important spokesman for the state party to the Jeffersonian administration. As a result, his was a strong voice in dispensing patronage in the state. He wrote to President Jefferson, outlining New Jersey's priorities under the new national administration, and Jefferson chided him for his long shopping list: "It is the case of one loaf and ten men wanting bread." But Bloomfield delivered federal offices in 1801 and thereafter, and Jefferson seldom treated him lightly.

In his day, in point of ability he has been compared with Alexander Hamilton, the great leader of the Federalists. As a general of militia he was called into service to take part in quelling the Whiskey Insurrection in Pennsylvania. Joseph Bloomfield was a longtime leader of the New Jersey Society for the Abolition of Slavery, and as governor, Bloomfield used his moral and political

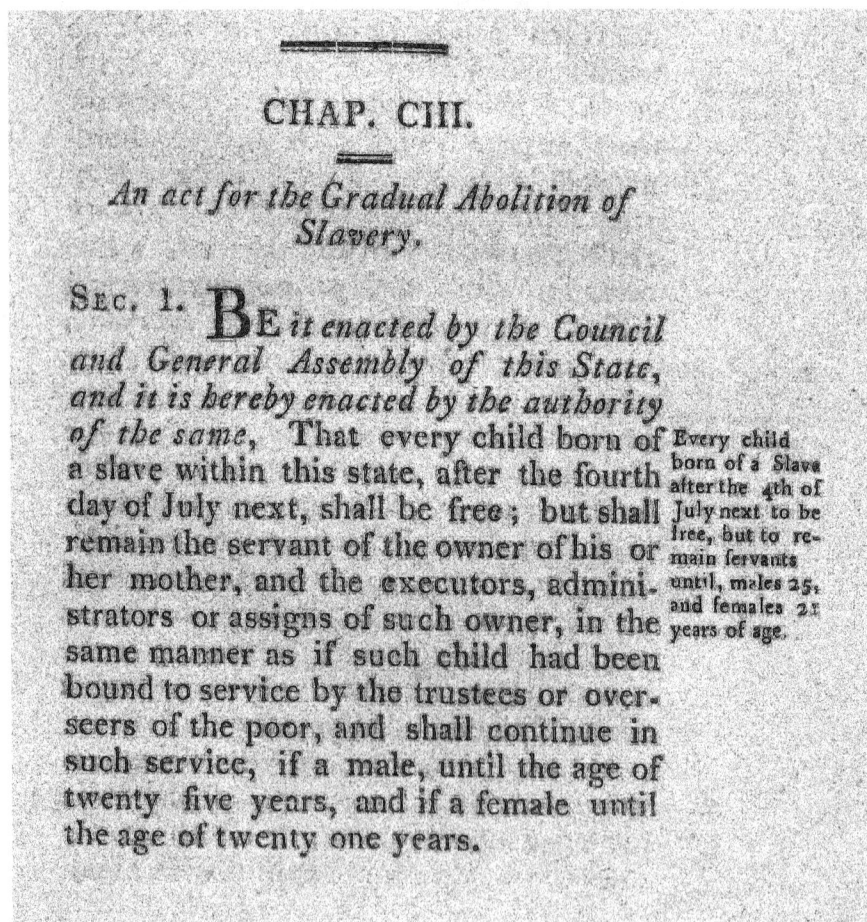

CHAP. CIII.

An act for the Gradual Abolition of Slavery.

SEC. 1. BE it enacted by the Council and General Assembly of this State, and it is hereby enacted by the authority of the same, That every child born of a slave within this state, after the fourth day of July next, shall be free; but shall remain the servant of the owner of his or her mother, and the executors, administrators or assigns of such owner, in the same manner as if such child had been bound to service by the trustees or overseers of the poor, and shall continue in such service, if a male, until the age of twenty five years, and if a female until the age of twenty one years.

Every child born of a Slave after the 4th of July next to be free, but to remain servants until, males 25, and females 21 years of age.

Title page from the Gradual Emancipation Act of 1804. *Courtesy Peter Mazzei, New Jersey Office of Legislative Services.*

leadership to initiate the gradual emancipation of slavery in New Jersey. In 1804 he signed the Gradual Emancipation Act, which steadily reduced the slave population of New Jersey from six percent of the total population in 1800 to eighteen individuals by 1860.

A potent lobbyist, Bloomfield was instrumental in promoting a considerable measure of Republican unity against slavery. Although he was accused of turning his back on his elite ties and background, he also favored controversial legislative reform measures to tax dividends from private bank stock and the creation of state-chartered banks to thwart monopolistic private banking interests in New Jersey.

THE WAR OF 1812

The rivalries and wars of European powers had enabled the United States to establish its independence. Separation from British sovereignty had made it possible to escape participation in the wars of the French Revolution and the Napoleonic Wars (1803-1815). Europe's distresses had given Jefferson the chance in 1803 to double the territory of the United States with the procurement of the Louisiana Territory. Negotiations had dragged on for almost two years when suddenly war was declared on France by Great Britain. More to embarrass Great Britain than to accommodate the United States, Napoleon decided to sell the entire Louisiana Territory for $15,000,000.00, a little less than four cents an acre.

In 1803 Jefferson, with almost no U.S. Navy, had little choice than to resort to economic warfare. In December, 1807, Jefferson ordered a complete British embargo. However by 1812 the United States found itself aligned on the side of Napoleon, the autocrat of Europe, against Great Britain. The ever-living question of neutral rights, including impressments, combined with the expansionist sentiment of the new American West, compelled the country to war. Western "War Hawks" dreamed of the conquest of Canada, while southern and southwestern states hoped for the conquest and seizure of Florida from Great Britain's feeble ally, Spain.

During his last years in office, 1808 to 1812, Bloomfield—like Republican officeholders everywhere—was caught up in defending unpopular foreign policy measures emanating from Washington. In an effort to protect American sovereignty while keeping the nation out of war with England, the Jefferson and Madison administrations had introduced successive measures embargoing trade with England, inevitably interrupting commerce with all of Europe. The consequent economic recession in the United States and the popular emotional reactions to continuing impressments of American sailors on the high seas placed New Jersey's Republicans on the defensive and caused a division in party ranks. Bloomfield contended expertly with these political difficulties, defending his party against allegations that it was "the party of war."

Jeffersonian Democratic-Republicans were hopelessly divided by foreign policy questions. They revitalized Federalists. Even so Bloomfield managed to gain reelection in the joint meeting of the legislature each October. When war was finally declared in June 1812, Bloomfield promptly resigned as governor in midterm to accept President Madison's nomination on March 24, 1812, as brigadier general in the rapidly expanding United States Army. His main task was to supervise the training and organizing of the defenses of New York and Pennsylvania. His brigade reached Sacketts Harbor, New York in 1813, but its commanding officer was soon transferred to the command of a military district with headquarters at Philadelphia, where he remained until peace was declared. As mentioned, General Zebulon Montgomery Pike also distinguished himself during the War of 1812.

With the state and nation facing another war with Great Britain, New Jersey Federalists rode a peace platform to victory in the fall of 1812. Federalists

Damage to the U.S. Capitol building after the burning of Washington by the British. *Illustration by George Munger.*

Zebulon Montgomery Pike. *Wikipedia; Creative Commons License*

pulled together a variety of anti-war elements—the sincere pacifist Quakers of West Jersey and the industrialists and merchants of East Jersey—who felt war with Great Britain would bring commercial disaster, and so it did. New Jersey voters backed peace in 1812 despite the fact that the war had already begun. Voters backed peace so overwhelmingly that Federalists controlled both houses of the legislature and swept Aaron Ogden into the governor's seat.

James Lawrence depicted on faux-scrimshaw. *Author's collection.*

The U.S.S. *Chesapeake* depicted on faux-scrimshaw. *Author's collection.*

Governor Ogden called the attention of his Federalist Legislature to the state's unpreparedness and in January 1813, urged stepped-up training of the militia. More than 6,000 New Jersey men were called into action. Great Britain, however, did establish an effective blockade off the Jersey coast in 1813, thwarting the commercial interest of the richest commercial enterprises of the United States, Philadelphia and New York, with France and its allies. But war was far away, in Canada or the burning of Washington.

New Jersey's chief memory of the War of 1812 came from the first rate hero it gave to the nation: Captain James Lawrence. Son of the mayor of the port town of Burlington, Judge John Lawrence, "Captain Jim" was born in 1781 in the Lawrence house at the corner of Main and Library Streets. Years later this same house became the residence of Joseph Bloomfield.

Seventeen years her junior, James was the half-brother of Elizabeth Lawrence, better known to the literary world of her day as "Madame Scribblerus." She married Michael Kearny of Perth Amboy, New Jersey in 1774. They lived at the Kearny Cottage where they raised both James Lawrence and their son Lawrence Kearny, the sailor-diplomat responsible for initiating relations between the United States and China in the early 1840s.

The young Perth Amboy skipper James Lawrence's succession of victories earned him the command of the forty-eight-gun frigate U.S.S. *Chesapeake* in 1813. It clashed in a fierce broadside combat with the British ship *Shannon* off Boston Harbor on June 3, 1813. Midway in the battle a bullet tore through Lawrence's body. As he was carried below, he delivered the now well-known command, "Don't give up the ship!" It became the battle cry of the fleet. Four days later Captain Jim died in Halifax, Nova Scotia.

CONCLUSION

The town of Bloomfield, New Jersey, formerly known as Wardsesson, received its present name in October, 1796 when the local Presbyterian congregation decided to honor Major General Joseph Bloomfield by naming the church the Bloomfield Presbyterian Church. On July 6, 1797, General Bloomfield and his wife visited the congregation, and he contributed $140 to the building fund and Mrs. Bloomfield presented a Bible printed in Trenton, New Jersey in 1791. Sixteen years later the town of Bloomfield was established. Thus, according to author Ellis L. Derry, the town was named for the church and not the church for the town, which is a rare distinction. Montclair, Belleville, Glen Ridge, and Nutley have all been formed from the twenty square miles that once was Bloomfield, and Bloomfield College was later established in 1860.

When the war ended in 1815, General Bloomfield retired to his mansion in Burlington. His ease was short-lived; his personal popularity and ability to unite warring factions of the party resulted in his election to two terms in the House of Representatives, in 1816 and 1818, the same year that his wife Mary passed away. As was appropriate, he was placed at the head of the Committee on Revolutionary Claims, and owing to his energy and perseverance, introduced and caused to be enacted bills granting pensions to Revolutionary War soldiers and their widows.

Only in 1820, in his sixty-seventh year, was he allowed to decline renomination and retire again to his estate in South Jersey. He married once more; his second wife was Isabella Ramsay Macomb. There were no children from either marriage. He died at Burlington, New Jersey, on October 3, 1823, overshadowed in history by the Founding Fathers, to whom he was contemporary, but bound to them by his able service to the causes that had rendered them immortal. Joseph Bloomfield is buried in old St.

Mary's Churchyard, Burlington, New Jersey as is patriot Elias Boudinot, who served as President of the Continental Congress.

Joseph Bloomfield was a popular hero of the Revolutionary War, a devoted Christian, and an active member of the New Jersey Bible Society. He was a member of the Presbyterian Church during an era when that church, in its entirety, was staunchly evangelical in its theology. Those evangelical Christian moral convictions were a driving force in his lifelong efforts to end the immoral institution of slavery.

On March 27, 1776, Captain Joseph Bloomfield, along with a company of sixty-five men from Cumberland County, left Bridgeton. In his journal Lieutenant Ebenezer Elmer wrote, describing some points of Bloomfield's character, "Captain Bloomfield, active, unsteady, fond of show, and a great admirer of his own abilities; quick passions, but easily pacified."

Bloomfield managed to combine the roles of governor and party leader during his long tenure in office and remained a powerful figure in New Jersey for nearly a quarter of a century. Nearly two centuries after his death, Joseph Bloomfield is out of fashion, too remote in time and temperament to engage our emotions. When Emerson declared, "Every hero becomes a bore at last," he may have had Joseph Bloomfield on his mind.

EPILOGUE

Preserving the history and rich heritage of Woodbridge Township is critical for the ages. Those who came before us and those who will continue after us deserve to know who was responsible for settling and building this vibrant, historic community, the oldest chartered township in the state of New Jersey.

The Bloomfield family has held its place in Woodbridge Township since 1667. Settled in Woodbridge, the family remained there for many years, and their family home still remains on Harrell Avenue. The story of Joseph Bloomfield is an interesting and exciting one. Not only did he serve his country; he served his state as well. His governorship ran from 1801-1812, an accomplishment for which Woodbridge should be very proud. He participated in many of the Revolutionary War battles fought in New Jersey, and dedicated his life to the cause he represented.

Donald Johnstone Peck has dedicated his life to researching and writing about the many historically significant people, places, and events that have made Woodbridge Township important to the state of New Jersey and the United States of America. His commitment, perseverance, and love of history is second to none and likened to the dedication of historian, Arthur M. Shlessinger, Jr., and Denis Diderot, co-founder, chief editor and contributor of the first *Encyclopedia* over the course of 1751-1777, and whose works have helped to preserve history through the generations.

Woodbridge Township congratulates and commends Donald Johnstone Peck for his untiring efforts to "get it all down on paper" for the coming generations.

Dolores Capraro Gioffre, Ed.D.
Woodbridge Township Historic Preservation Chair

BIBLIOGRAPHY

BOOKS

Barber, John W., and Henry Howe. *Historical Collections of the State of New Jersey*. Newark, N.J.: Benjamin Olds for Justus H. Bradley, 1844.

Beck, Henry Carlton. *More Forgotten Towns of Southern New Jersey*. New Brunswick, N.J.: Rutgers University Press, 1963.

Bemis, Samuel Flagg. *A Diplomatic History of the United States*. New York, N.Y.: Henry Holt and Company, 1955.

Bilby, Joseph G., and Katherine Bilby Jenkins. *Monmouth Court House The Battle That Made The American Army*. Yardley, P.A.: Westholme Publishing, LLC, 2010.

Bill, Alfred Hoyt. *New Jersey and the Revolutionary War*. New Brunswick, N.J.: Rutgers University Press, 1964.

Birkner, Michael J., and Paul A. Stellhorn. *The Governors of New Jersey*. Trenton, N.J.: New Jersey Historical Commission, 1982.

Bond, Gordon. *A Printer on the Eve of Revolution*. Morristown, N.J.: New Jersey History Press, 2008

Brookhiser, Richard. *Founding Father*. New York, N.Y.: Simon & Schuster, 1996.

Brady, Patricia. *Martha Washington: An America Life*. New York, N.Y.: Penguin Books, 2006.

Chadwick, Bruce. *Triumvirate*. New York, N.Y.: Fall River Press, 2009.

Chernow, Ron. *Alexander Hamilton*. New York, N.Y.: The Penguin Press, 2004.

Cunningham, John T. *New Jersey: America's Main Road*. Garden City, N.Y.: Doubleday and Company, 1966.

Derry, Ellis L. *Old and Historic Churches of New Jersey*. Union City, N.J.; Wm. H. Wise & Company, 1979.

Di Ionno, Mark. *A Guide To New Jersey's Revolutionary War Trails For Families And History Buffs*. New Brunswick, N.J.: Rutgers University Press, 2000.

Farmer, Thomas P. *New Jersey In History Fighting To Be Heard*. Harvey Cedars, N.J.: Down the Shore Publishing Corp., 1996.

Lefkowitz, Arthur S. *The Long Retreat: The Calamitous American Defense of New Jersey 1776*. New Brunswick, N.J.: Rutgers University Press, 1999.

McCormick, Richard P. *New Jersey From Colony to State – 1609-1789*. Princeton, N.J.: D. Van Nostrand Company, Inc., 1964.

McGinnis, William Carroll. *History of Perth Amboy, New Jersey 1651-1960 Vol. III*. Perth Amboy, N.J.: American Publishing Company, 1960.

McGuire, Thomas J. *Stop the Revolution*. Mechanicsburg, PA.: Stackpole Books, 2011.

Miers, Earl Schenck. *Where the Raritan Flows*. New Brunswick, N.J.: Rutgers University Press, 1964.

Mills, W. Jay. *Historic Houses of New Jersey*. Union City, N.J.: William H. Wise & Company, Inc., 1977.

New Jersey Guild Associates, Inc. *New Jersey: A Guide to Its Present And Past.* New York, N.Y.: Hastings House, 1939.

Peck, Donald Johnstone. *A Spirited War, George Washington and the Ghosts of the Revolution in Central New Jersey.* Franklin, TN.: American History Imprints, 2009.
-----*An American Journey of Hope.* Staunton, VA.: American History Press, 2013.

Pierce, Arthur D. *Smugglers' Woods.* New Brunswick, N.J.: Rutgers University Press, 1960.

Prince, Carl E. *New Jersey's Jeffersonian Republicans, 1789-1817.* Chapel Hill, N.C.: University of North Carolina Press, 1967.

Randall, Willard Sterne, and Nancy Nahra. *Forgotten Americans.* Cambridge, MA.: Perseus Publishing, 1999.

Rosenfeld, Richard N. American Aurora: *A Democratic-Republican Returns: The Suppressed History of Our Nation's Beginnings and the Heroic Newspaper That Tried to Report it.* New York, N.Y.: St. Martin's Press, 1997.

Smith, Richard Norton. *Patriarch, George Washington and the New American Nation.* New York, N.Y.: Houghton Mifflin Company, 1993.

Troeger, Virginia Bergen and Robert J. McEwen. *Woodbridge New Jersey's Oldest Township.* Charleston, S.C.: Arcadia Publishing, 2002.

Wall, John P. and Harold E. Pickersgill. *History of Middlesex County New Jersey 1664-1920.* New York, N.Y.: Lewis Historical Publishing Company. Inc., Vol. 1 and 2, 1921.

Whitehead, William A., *Contributions to the Early History of Perth Amboy and Adjoining Country with Sketches of Men and Events in New Jersey During the Provincial Era.* New York: D. Appleton & Company, 1856.

MONOGRAPHS

Becker, Ronald L. *"A Republican Meeting in Burlington County – 1800."* New Jersey History, Summer, 1974 Quarterly, The New Jersey Historical Society. 1974.

Cowan, Thomas D. "Philip Freneau: The Artist in the Early Republic." New Jersey History, Winter, 1774 Quarterly, The New Jersey Historical Society. 1974.

Demarest, William H.S. *"George Washington: An Appreciation."* The Washington Association of New Jersey, Washington's Headquarters In Morristown, N.J. 1942.

Fleming, Thomas. *"Springfield – The Reason Why."* New Jersey History, Winter, 1974 Quarterly, The New Jersey Historical Society. 1974.

Geissler, Suzanne B. *"The Burr-Hamilton Duel and Related Matters."* New Jersey History, Winter, 1972 Quarterly, The New Jersey Historical Society. 1973.

Gerlach, Larry R. *"William Franklin: New Jersey's Last Royal Governor."* New Jersey's Revolutionary Experience, New Jersey Historical Commission. 1975.

I. N. Phelps Stokes. "New York Past and Present: It's History and Landmarks 1524-1939." Plantin Press, N.Y., 1939

INDEX

ABOUT THE AUTHOR

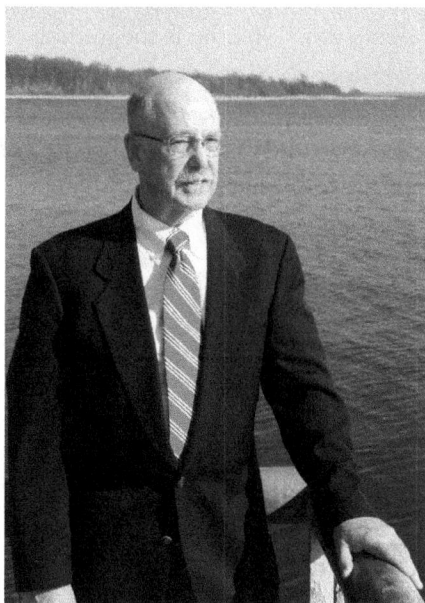

Donald Johnstone Peck is an alumnus of Earlham College, Richmond, Indiana, Class of 1961, with a major in history and French, including studies at the University of Paris, France, 1960.

Professionally, he is the President and CEO of The Clausen Company, Inc., Fords, New Jersey, established in 1957, a leading manufacturer of automotive refinishing products for the automotive aftermarket, and Past President of the National Association of Autobody Filler Manufacturers, 1983-86.

Non-professionally, he is Trustee for the League of New Jersey Historical Societies; immediate Past President of the Raritan-Millstone Heritage Alliance, Inc., Somerset, New Jersey; past commissioner for the Woodbridge Historic Preservation Commission, Woodbridge, New Jersey, President Emeritus of the Proprietary House Association, Perth Amboy, New Jersey and Founding Member and past vice president of the Colt's Neck Historical Society, Colts Neck, New Jersey.

A direct descendant of six signers of the Mayflower Compact, he has active memberships in The Society of Mayflower Descendants in the State of New Jersey and several state and national historical organizations. A direct descendant of Elisha Parker, Sr., progenitor of the illustrious Parker Family

ABOUT THE AUTHOR

of Woodbridge and Perth Amboy, he also descends from Sir George Scott and Dr. John Johnstone, proprietors of East Jersey.

A recipient of the Episcopal Diocese of Newark Commission On Aging Lifetime Achievement Award, in recognition of the many contributions to church and community, he is a long–term preservationist currently restoring the buildings, gardens and grounds at Olde Stone Cottage, at the site of the historic Cutter Farm, Fords, New Jersey.

Co-author of *The History of Colts Neck, New Jersey,* 1964, he is the author of *A Spirited War: George Washington and the Ghosts of the Revolution in Central New Jersey,* 2009, *An American Journey Of Hope: Perth Amboy, The Capital and Port City on Raritan Bay*, 2013, and numerous monographs and essays published in *The Link*, the quarterly publication of the Raritan-Millstone Heritage Alliance.

www.ingramcontent.com/pod-product-compliance
Lightning Source LLC
Chambersburg PA
CBHW070332090426
42733CB00012B/2452